CHINESE PRACTICES
AND BELIEFS

CHINESE PRACTICES AND BELIEFS

WRITTEN AND ILLUSTRATED BY

Evelyn Lip PH.D.

**MASTERS IN ARCHITECTURE
DIPARCH (LONDON)**

HEIAN

Revised American Edition 2000
10 9 8 7 6 5 4 3 2 1

Heian International, Inc
1815 West 205th Street Suite #301
Torrance CA 90501

E-mail: heianemail@heian.com
Web site: www.heian.com

ISBN:0-89346-928-9

Printed by Dominie Press—Singapore

Dedicated to my beloved and filial children,
Yau Sueng (Kenny) and Tzun Cheang (Jacqueline)

Contents

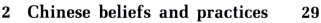

Preface

If I were asked to describe Chinese culture in a few words I would say it is indeed a many splendoured thing. Chinese culture has enriched the lives of people living outside as well as within China for centuries, and is likely to continue to do so for many future generations. Chinese cultural development, spanning several thousand years of history, has proven remarkably enduring. Students researching its origins may find that its many forms take a lifetime to understand fully. Chinese traditions are still observed within and, even more so, outside China as overseas Chinese cling to their cultural heritage. To what extent are these practices followed? How do the Chinese celebrate birth and marriage? Are traditional festivals still observed? What religious beliefs still influence their lives? What is feng shui and how does it enhance the placement of buildings? Why are Chinese buildings decorated with so many symbols? What makes Chinese calligraphy and brush painting so unique? How do we appreciate Chinese opera and art? What is yin or yang food and when do we need it? What is the fundamental Chinese theory behind the use of herbal medicine? These questions are constantly being asked by people of Chinese origin as well as by foreign scholars. This book attempts to give an overview of Chinese culture and its colourful spectrum.

The introduction and Chapter 1 present the Chinese concept of society, important events and festivals. The second chapter describes religious beliefs and practices such as martial arts. The third explains the fascinating theory of yin and yang and the five elements, which is central to Chinese thinking. Chinese architecture and landscaping are presented in Chapter 4. The various forms of Chinese art ranging from brush painting to tea drinking are introduced in Chapter 5. In Chapter 6 Chinese opera and musical instruments are described and illustrated. Finally, the way the Chinese seek to prolong life is discussed in Chapter 7.

Foreword

It was Confucius' celebrated pupil Zeng Zi (曾子) who said that on the grounds of culture one meets friends (以文会友). It is out of a friendship of this nature that I write the foreword for Dr Evelyn Lip's book *Chinese Practices and Beliefs*.

Like the skilled weaving maiden in the Chinese legend Dr Lip has woven the five-thousand-year-old landscape of Chinese culture into a single picture. This masterpiece may be devoured in a sitting but it is better to read at leisure. Take time to study the fine calligraphy section; savour the sections on food and medicine. Pause and enjoy each concisely written topic each thread running through the tapestry that depicts our Chinese heritage.

Chinese Practices and Beliefs is a book for the eye, the mind, the heart and the soul. There is much to please the eye in the rich illustrations and photographs; there is much to think about in the many ideas presented; and there is much to prompt reminiscence, especially for older folks who may be reminded of places and experiences dear to their hearts. Who does not remember the excitement of putting on a new outfit or pair of shoes at Chinese New Year, or the taste of their favourite food?

Poetry lovers will be delighted by the poems quoted at the beginning of each chapter. My own favourite is Qing Ming (清明) by Du Mu (杜牧), about the traditional practice of visiting ancestral graves and paying respects with offerings in the spring.

This is a book for people of all ages. It will remind the old of their youth; the middle aged of their heritage; and it will encourage the young to search for their cultural roots. All said, Dr Evelyn's book is a compendium of Chinese culture and traditions, worth having in the family.

Wu Teh Yao
former Dean, College of Graduate Studies, Nanyang University and Professor of Political Science, University of Singapore.

Introduction

秋 夕
qiū xī

杜 牧
dù mù

This poem was one of Du Mu's poems and was written during the Tang period. It describes the beauty of an autumn night and the weather under the glitter of the stars, representing the romance of the Weaving Lady and the Cowherd.

银	烛	秋	光	冷	画	屏，
yín	zhú	qiū	guāng	lěng	huà	píng
轻	罗	小	扇	扑	流	萤。
qīng	luó	xiǎo	shàn	pū	liú	yíng
天	阶	夜	色	凉	如	水，
tiān	jiē	yè	sè	liáng	rú	shuǐ
坐	看	牵	牛	织	女	星。
zuò	kàn	qiān	niú	zhī	nǚ	xīng

China is a vast country with a long and interesting history and a tremendously rich culture, art and architecture. The evidence records a cultural development spanning thousands of years. As far back as the 16th century BC the casting of bronze, the carving of jade and the art of lacquering were already relatively advanced. In 1120 BC Chinese chess was invented as a mimic warfare. By that time the ruler of the Zhou had also established a system of horoscopes. As early as the 11th century BC building techniques and other artforms had already begun to develop.

The ancient Chinese worshipped all sorts of deities and in the 6th and 7th centuries BC they accepted the philosophies of Confucius and Lao Zi. These philosophies influenced the many aspects of Chinese culture, including natural sciences, architectural and furniture design, and social practices. Confucian thinking moulded the planning of houses, palaces and temples while Lao Zi's Daoism reinforced the central Chinese thinking on harmony of yin and yang and on the balance of the five elements of Gold, Wood, Water, Fire and Earth. The theory of yin and yang was, and still is applied, to the naming of a newborn child.

The cultivation of the art of painting dates back to before the 6th century while porcelain making as an artform, started as early as the 7th century AD. Chinese cultural achievements in the arts have developed over thousands of years and have been handed down to the present day. One of the earlier works on poems and songs, edited by Confucius, the Shijing, reflected the culture of the ancient society and formed the foundation of song writing. There is evidence that poetic composition dates from over six thousand years ago, as reflected on ancient porcelain wares. Chinese characters and text have been found on oracle bones and tortoise shells five thousand years old. Portrait and landscape painting were perfected over the many dynasties and became a distinctive form of artistic expression. This cultural heritage is still being preserved all over the world by people of Chinese origin, perhaps partly because many of these cultural practices such as brush painting, calligraphy and feng shui are means of nourishing and cultivating not just the spirit but also the physical well being of man.

Temple at the Yihe Yuan, Beijing

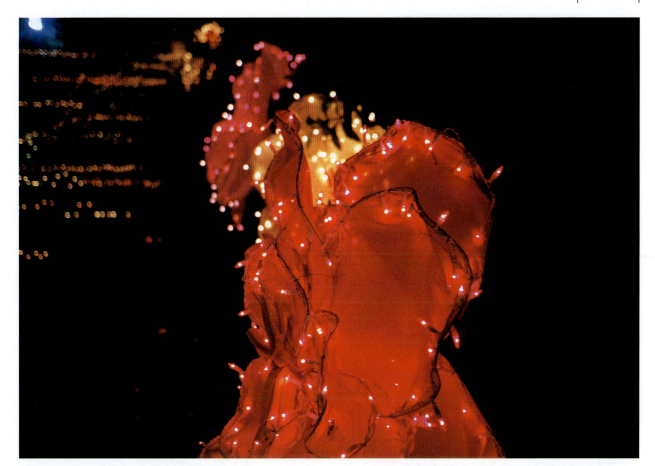

Light Lantern of various sizes and forms are displayed during the Moon Festival

The last five thousand years of Chinese cultural history is spectacularly rich, manifesting itself in philosophy and classics, arts and architecture, music and performing arts, religious practices and beliefs, martial arts and literary pursuits, eating and drinking and life itself, and is so multi-faceted that it is impossible to cover every aspect of it. It has influenced every facade of life and every form of art. It pervades the organisation of Chinese society and institutions, in the architecture of both domestic and religious buildings, in the written text of Chinese philosophy and science.

Millions of Chinese emigrated to other parts of the world, especially during the internal turmoil of the Qing dynasty just before the formation of the People's Republic of China. These immigrants brought their culture, social structure, religions, arts and technological skills to the foreign lands in which they settled

yin ding 银锭 *representing wealth.*

gui wen 龟文 *representing longevity.*

shi liu 石榴 *representing posterity.*

A calligrapher writing chunlian, New year greetings.

and although they began life anew they could not discard their cultural roots. They preserved the traditional values they had acquired in their homeland and passed them down to their children.

In many parts of the world today, ethnic Chinese have acquired citizenship of their adopted lands and even though they may be of the third generation to be born in that place they still practise their forefathers' cultural and social customs. These customs have evolved over time but they are still easily recognisable as Chinese in origin. The objective of this book is to present the various cultural and social practices of the overseas Chinese which are still practised outside China. Most of the practices described in this book are now universally known although some, such as Kan Yu or Feng Shui, are jealously guarded skills, and are known only to a privileged few. These are examined in separate sections.

Animal symbols.

Acknowledgements

First and Foremost I would like to thank the late professor Wu The-yao, the former Dean, College of Graduate Studies, Nanyang University and Professor of Political Science, University of Singapore, for writing the foreword of this book. Professor Wu was a well-known and respected Confucian scholar and he was the author of *The Confucian Way* and *Roots of Chinese Culture*. This book contains many aspects of Chinese culture and naturally, historical records alone proved insufficient for my research. Many live interviews had to be conducted. I wish to express my gratitude to the following people who have in some way or other given me advice and enlightenment during the interviews:

To Mrs. Wang-Lee Tee Eng, Managing Director of the Hong Reng Tang Imperial Kitchen (S) Pte Ltd., for her advice on herbal food;

TO Mr. Li Lian Xing, herbalist and Chinese Physician, for his help in selecting the herbs for various cures;

To Michelle, Managing Director of Yi Hu Xuan Tea House, for her demonstration of the art of tea ceremony;

To Mr. Tony Tong, former Managing Director of Sunrise Scdn Bhd., for his permission to use the perpectives of Mont Kiara, Palma, Kuala Lumpur, to demonstrate the present day application of a building with good feng shui;

To Mrs. Joanna Wong, an internationally-known, celebrated and accomplished Chinese opera artist, for her pemission to publish her photographs in this book and for her valuable advice;

1  Ancient Chinese society, celebrations and important events

新嫁娘

xīn   jià   niáng

王 建

wáng jiàn

三 日 入 厨 下,
sān rì rù chú xià

洗 手 作 羹 汤。
xǐ shǒu zuò gēng tāng

未 谙 姑 食 性,
wèi ān gū shí xìng

先 遣 小 姑 尝。
xiān qiǎn xiǎo gū cháng

Wang Jian, a Tang dynasty poet, relates the traditional practice of the bride going to the kitchen on the third day to cook. Apprehensive of not pleasing her mother-in-law, she asks her sister-in-law to taste the food before serving it.

CONTENTS

1.1 | Chinese immigration

The cultural connections between China and Southeast Asia can be traced back to the 15th century when Zheng He 郑和, a Ming dynasty statesman, made a trip to the "South Seas". From 1664 onwards, when the Manchus overcame the Ming dynasty in China, constant warfare in South China reinforced the tendency to emigrate. Those who did leave belonged to a number of different dialect groups and moved to the Southeast Asian countries in order to find work, aiming to return with their savings. By the early 19th century, they were arriving in great numbers, principally from the Southern provinces of Guangdong and Fujian.

The society of immigrant Chinese during the early 19th century was fairly close-knit. However, the mixture of dialect groups resulted in conflicts of interest, and the situation was exacerbated by there being no proper authorities to deal with their social welfare. Community leaders, belonging to the merchant class, did what they could to unite the people of each dialect group by forming clan associations and community centres for social gatherings and meetings, and recruited more immigrants under the Indenture System. Through these the migrants had their passages to Singapore and other Southeast Asian countries, their food and clothing paid for in return for their labour. The richest and possibly largest dialect groups were the Fujian and Guangdong migrants. They built Chinese temples as association centres and clan associations. Those who had made their fortunes in tin mining, opium and liquor distilling, for example, were strongly motivated to make generous donations to temple building funds. The maintenance of traditional values was an important reason for them to make contributions to the social welfare of the less fortunate. By the mid 20th century the Chinese migrants had firmly established their position and consequently needed to look less to their motherland for moral support and spiritual guidance. The Revolution in China in 1948 was the final determining factor: emigration from the mainland was stopped by the authorities and, thus all forms of intercourse ceased. As a result, the importance attached to kinship and to clan membership has lessened substantially. The clan associations still exist for reasons of clan unity and ancestor worship, albeit in a diluted form.

1.2 | Families and clans

The organisation of Chinese society and the Chinese political system from the 6th century BC to the Qing dynasty were greatly influenced by the teachings of Confucius, a 6th century BC philosopher who taught the meaning of ren 仁 (magnanimity), yi 义 (righteousness) and dao de 道德 (virtue). Confucius advocated that a man should treat others as he wished to be treated himself. In the past scholars studied the Four Books: *The Book of Great Learning, The Doctrine of the Mean, The Analects* and *The Book of Mencius*; and the Six Classics: *The Book of Changes, The Book of History, The Book of Odes, The Annals of Spring and Autumn, The Book of Rites* and *The Book of Music*. These books and classics were based on the teaching of Confucius and his disciples and they formed the foundation of Chinese society.

In old Chinese society there was a well-defined place for each person. For example, in a family the head of the household was the oldest male who was responsible for the well being of his entire family. If he was reasonably wealthy he was to provide shelter and food to his extended family and in return he commanded respect and obedience. His wife, who was in charge of the household, would not be expected to earn an income. In a family unit the father looked after his son's welfare while the son gave his respect in return. Brothers were expected to be united and friends trustworthy. It was taken for granted that everyone would be loyal to his country because without a country there would be no family. Chinese community was centred around the extended family, comprising parents, children and relatives. Each member of the extended family had a definite place and a role to play. People in the same province formed an association, people of

the same surname joined a clan and people of the same trade organised a trade guild.

In old Chinese society the reputation and honour of a family were very important. If someone broke the law he would disgrace his entire extended family. If a member of a clan or association did a disgraceful act he would be judged by the entire clan and his punishment would be pronounced by the clan leader. For example, if a man and a woman were found guilty of adultery they would be encaged and drowned together.

The father's property was inherited by his sons because only males could perpetuate the family name. Once a girl had grown up and married she had to take her husband's surname and would immediately be regarded as an outsider. If a man had no sons his fortune would be inherited by his brother's sons. Even his own wife, who might have borne him 10 daughters, could not inherit her marital home. In such a decadent society the resulting intrigue and complicated family politics often ended in tragedy. Fortunately, this practice has been discontinued since the start of the 20th century.

The original functions and activities of clan associations in the Southeast Asian regions were:

1) to house and feed new immigrants;
2) to help immigrants find jobs;
3) to settle disputes among the clan members and dialect groups;
4) to arrange for immigrants to return to mainland China; and

5) to raise funds to build more association centres, temples and to send funds to relieve major national calamities in China.

Clan associations or huiguan 会馆 were set up for almost every dialect group, including the Fujian Huiguan, the Guangdong Huiguan, the Hainan, and the Fuzhou Huiguan. The Fujian Huiguan was the most wealthy in Singapore and in some states of Malaysia e.g. Penang. Some prominent personalities of the Fujian Huiguan have reached the highest rank in Chinese Society e.g. Mr Tan Lark Sye and Mr Wee Cho Yaw.

Some of the early leaders of clan associations were handicapped by their illiteracy and hence, they promoted education and set up schools for the education of the children of clan members. This function still exists today in some clan associations, and scholarships and bursary schemes are available for needy students.

Clan associations are organised and managed by an executive council comprising as many as 40 members working under a Chairman. Committees are formed to deal with all kinds of general affairs, such as finance, social welfare and education.

1.3 | Etiquette

Chinese protocol and etiquette were extremely elaborate in ancient times. Confucius advocated the virtues of diligence, kindness and protocol of the Qin period in the *Liji* 礼制. He stressed that between the ruler and his subjects, courtesy and compiled the court eti-

quette and between man and wife as well as between a man and his compatriots there must be respect. There was a correct way of behaving and of approaching others. Codes of practice and behaviour were written to help court officials of every rank and people from all walks of life to behave in a civilised manner. A man could be beheaded if he violated the code of practice before a high official or a ruler.

Codes of behaviour were also written in old classics. A woman was supposed to uphold her virtue and to stay in her home; to be seen but not heard. She was to practise san cong 三从 (the three obediences) namely zai jia cong fu 在家从父 (obey the father before marriage), chu

Tong Shu 通书 *The Tongshu, the Chinese Almanac, contains lunar activities that bring in good consequences and auspicious qi.*

jia cong fu 出嫁从夫 (obey the husband after marriage), and lao lai cong zi 老来从子 (obey the son in old age). A special classical record on the etiquette of girls named *Nu Er Jing* 女儿经 was read by all unmarried women of good families. The *Tong Shu* 通书 (a Chinese almanac) still publishes the classical essay of Zeng Guang Xian Wen 增广贤文 which reflects the nature of man. In it are some rules on social etiquette. For example, the saying "ning ke ren fu wo, qie mo wo fu ren...yi yan ji chu, si ma nan zhui" 宁可人负我, 切莫我负人…一言既出, 驷马难追 (let others disappoint me but let me not disappoint others...once I have given my word even a fast horse cannot take it back) shows how important honour and trust were to a man of honour and how he was supposed to behave in society. A classical writing named *Zhi Jia Ge Yan* 治家格言 was published specially for men on how to manage a home and family. Aphorisms taught how a man should regard material things in life; how he should bring up the younger generation; how he should treat relatives, aged parents, the poor and the rich. Powers were not to be misused, one was not to take pleasure in another's failures and harmony was to be sustained in one's home.

As mentioned earlier the attitude of a man towards his fellow men should be based on ren 仁 (magnanimity) and yi 义 (trust and honour). The word ren 仁 (magnanimity) is written with two Chinese characters, ren 人 (man) and er 二 (two) reflecting the importance to the Chinese of the concept of interdependence. Man should not try to exist like an island but

增广贤文

昔时贤文。诲汝谆谆。集韵增广。多见多闻。

观今宜鉴古。无古不成今。知己知彼。将心比心。

Part of Zeng Guang Xian Wen 增广贤文 *which reflects the nature of man.*

朱子治家格言
黎明即起，洒扫庭除要内外整洁
既昏便息，关锁门户必亲自检点。
一饭当思来处不易，半丝半缕恒念物
。

Part of Zhi Jia Ge Yan 治家格言 *which spells the art of managing a home.*

rather he is to relate with others in order to be accepted and to be successful in life. Thus the Chinese believe that it is worthwhile for a man to be humble and to give in to others who ask for favours otherwise he may hurt their feelings and be regarded as not giving them "face", or "tearing their faces". The face has always been regarded as one of the most important parts of the body and it is the metaphorical equivalent of the pride and honour of a man. If a man's pride is hurt he is said to have lost face and it is unthinkable for a man to lose face. Therefore, many proverbs have been written using the word "face" to represent feelings. For example, "mian bu gai se" 面不改色 means calmness and "mian hong er chi" 面红耳赤 (the face is red and the ear reddish) means blushing, either with shame or anger.

Cultural etiquette for a learned man includes the acquisition of various forms of arts such as playing a musical instrument, playing chess, writing and painting with a brush and ink, practising martial arts, reciting poems, singing and reading horoscopes. A cultured person must be alert, perceptive, respectful, curious and humble. He must not be boastful or use abusive language.

The Chinese have now discarded the old, decadent and strict protocol. But there are still certain basic rules of Chinese conduct that have survived the test of time and are being carried on as social courtesy. Because the Chinese have developed an exquisite cuisine and regard food as being most important in a man's life, they do not greet each other with "How are you?" but instead they ask, "Have you eaten?" This greeting is often given without a particular desire to know whether the person has eaten but rather whether he or she is feeling quite well.

The Chinese not only created countless ways of cooking but also invented chopsticks to eat with. The oldest chopsticks were found in a grave dating back to the 13th century BC. A pair of chopsticks can be made out of ivory, plastic, bamboo or wood.

Many traditional table manners are still observed today. It is best if the table used for a Chinese dinner is round. Once everyone is seated and the food is served the guests wait for the host to invite them to eat by saying "qi kuai" 起筷 (let us start to use the chopsticks). Some still practise calling the names of people dining with them as a form of courtesy. The bowl of rice is held with the left hand and brought close to the mouth while the rice is lifted into the mouth with the chopsticks which are held in the right hand. One should not make any noise when chewing the food. While waiting for the next course of food one should place the chopsticks neatly on the chopstick rest and avoid crossing them or putting them on the rice bowl. The spoon should not be used at the same time as the chopsticks. Toothpicks should not be used during the meal but rather at the end, and always whilst covering the mouth. Whenever tea is served one should say "thank you" or make a gesture of thanks. The etiquette of serving tea will be described in more detail in Chapter 5.

Whenever one attends a wedding dinner one should bring a present wrapped in colourful or reddish gift wrap (never black because it represents grief) or cash in a red packet (never in a white envelope because it is a colour for mourning). Presents must symbolise good luck or blessing such as gold pendants with symbols of luck (never a clock as the word for clock sounds like zhong 终, meaning die). When one is invited to a Chinese New Year party one should dress cheerfully (never completely in black because black is a solemn colour) and bring one's hosts oranges and new year red packet for luck and good wishes.

A Chinese red packet is printed in red which is an auspicious symbol. The red packet shows a ji 桔 *(a symbol of luck).*

The Chinese concept of "face" extends to the exchange of gifts. They believe that one should accept a good offer to give face and reciprocate accordingly. This means that if one receives presents from a friend or relative one should also give in return to show appreciation. The exchange of marriage gifts will be described later.

1.4 | Chinese values

Ancient Chinese values can be gleaned from the classical writings of Confucius and his disciples. The proper attitude towards one's fellow men, country, family, and home management as well as common wisdom on the value of learning and perseverance were contained in maxims, proverbs and sayings and handed down from one generation to another.

Some of these ancient teachings may be outdated but most of them are still applicable in a present day context. As soon as I was able to read my mother taught me recite the sayings contained in the Zeng Guang Xian Wen 增广贤文 which teaches Chinese values. On the subject of human relationships it advocates that one should treat others as one wishes to be treated. To get to know someone one has to be close to him, and one should not trust a stranger, for as the saying goes, "Zhi ren kou mian bu zhi xin 知人口面，不知心 (You may see the mouth and face but you cannot see the heart). Money is not everything but "love and trust" is worth a thousand pieces of gold. If there

is unity there is strength as "Liang ren yi ban xin, you qian kan mai jin. Yi ren yi ban xin, wu qian nan mai zhen"两人一般心，有钱堪买金。一人一般心，无钱难买针。(Two people with a united-heart can buy gold. Without a united heart they cannot even buy a needle).

With regard to education, one should seek knowledge as steadfastly as one is able and treat it as though it is as precious as gold. When one succeeds one will be well-known and well-rewarded as it says, "Shi nian chuang xia wu ren wen, yi zhao cheng ming tian xia zhi" 十年窗下无人问，一朝成名天下知 (No one spoke to him during the ten years he studied by the window. But the moment he succeeded in the imperial examination he was well-known to the whole world). Another saying that

The above picture depicts the Chinese saying: 'No one notices the scholar who studies for 10 years under the window'.

preaches the value of learning is, "Ji jin qian liang, bu ru ming jie jing shu. Yang zi bu jiao ru yang lu, yang nu bu jiao ru yang zhu" 积金千两，不如明解经书。养子不教如养驴，养女不教如养猪。(Having saved a thousand 0.05 kilogram measures of gold one does not feel as good as one does when one understands the classics. If one does not teach one's son during his upbringing one is likely to bring up a mule. To raise a daughter without educating her is like bringing up a pig).

One's attitude towards people one hardly knows should be cautious, as the saying goes, "Mo xin zhi zhong zhi, sui fang ren bu ren" 莫信直中直，虽防仁不仁 (Do not easily believe that someone is the most honest among the honest and beware of the most unethical of the unethical). This attitude is reinforced by another saying, "Shan zhong you zhi shu, shi shang wu zhi ren" 山中有直树，世上无直人 (There are straight trees on the hill, but no one on earth is completely honest).

About tolerance, the Chinese learn "Ren yi ju, xi yi nu. Rao yi zhao, tui yi bu." 忍一句，息一怒。饶一着，退一步。(Tolerate, listen to your sentence and control your temper. Not to claim righteousness is like retreating one step). The Chinese believe that good will triumph over evil as "Ren e ren pa, tian bu pa. Ren shan ren qi, tian bu qi" 人恶人怕，天不怕，人善人欺，天不欺。(Bullies are feared by man and not by God) and "Shan e dao tou zhong you bao, zhi zheng lai zao yu lai chi" 善恶到头终有报，只争来早与来迟。

This picture depicts the Chinese saying: 'Upright trees abound the hills but honest men are scarce and few'.

This picture depicts the Chinese saying: 'Dishonesty may never be reflected'.

The above picture depicts the Chinese saying, 'yang bing qian ri yong zai yi shi': 'An army is kept to fight a war'.

(The good and the evil will beget what they deserve although the timing may be early or late).

The Zeng Guang Xian Wen also preaches values with regard to one's attitude towards one's country and family. For example, it says, "Yang jun qian ri yong zai yi zhao" 养军千日用在一朝 (Feed the army for a thousand days for the use of it for one). This means that one has to perform one's duty when one is called upon to do so. "Guo qing cai zi gui, jia fu xiao er jiao" 国清才子贵，家富小儿骄 (When the administrators of the country are not corrupt, the educated feel proud. When the family is rich the children are treasured). "Fu zi he er jia bu tui. Xiong di he er jia bu fen" 父子和而家不退，兄弟和而家不分 (When the father and son live harmoniously the family will not degenerate. When the brothers live harmoniously they will not divide their inheritance).

The Zhi Jia Ge Yan 治家格言, the maxims of home management written during the 17th century by Zhu Bo Lu 朱柏卢, also teach man values with regard to learning, bringing up children and duties towards one's country. For example, the sayings: "Zi sun sui yu, jing shu bu ke bu du" 子孙虽愚，经书不可不读 (Even if the children are stupid, they must study the classics), "Jiao zi yao you yi fang" 教子要有义方 (Teach your children by the proper method), "Du shu zhi zai sheng xian" 读书志在圣贤 (Learn under wise teachers with principles), "Wei guan xin cun jun guo" 为官心存君国 (Government officers must be loyal to the ruler and country).

Chinese attitudes towards country and family have also been handed down through moral lessons and the heroic deeds of great warriors and wise rulers. For example, everyone has heard of the heroic deeds of the 12th century warrior, Yue Fei 岳飞 (1103–1142 AD) who won numerous wars and was most loyal to his country. His heroism was instilled in him by his mother who tattooed the words, "jin zhong bao guo" 尽忠报国 (try your very best to serve your country) on his back before he left home to serve in the army.

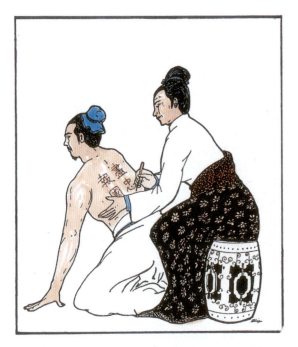

Yue Fei's mother tattoos on his back to remind him to be absolutely loyal to his country.

Perseverance and endurance are values that have been practised in China since time immemorial. The story about Yu Gong 愚公, who lived in a village blocked by two huge mountains, still inspires the young. Yu Gong tried to hack away the mountains to make a way to his house. His perseverance and determination touched the hearts of the gods who then helped him to achieve his ambition.

1.5 | Money and wealth

During the Han dynasty (206 BC–220 AD) gold and silver was used in China as a medium of exchange and means of payment for services and later, rolls of silk were also used. By the 9th century AD paper money was circulated in the form of money drafts and in certain areas in China steel coins were also used in addition to gold, silver and other precious metals, for the payment of goods and services. This practice was stopped by the Yuan rulers (from 1279 to 1368 AD) and so money printed in various denominations was used as a medium of exchange. One type was made with silk and the other with paper.

In old China there was a great difference in terms of wealth between the rich and the poor. The rich were aggressive and powerful while the poor weak and powerless. The rich became money lenders and charged huge compound interests for short term loans. Thus, it was said that a man was "you qian you mian" 有钱有面 (having money is having honour and respect) and "you qian neng shi gui tui che" 有钱能使鬼推车 (having money one can make the ghost drive one's chariot). Every man dreamt of becoming rich and thus the have-nots had to work extremely hard and save as much as possible. The rich accumulated wealth in the form of gold and silver as well as fixed assets such as real estate and farm land. Some of the very rich misused their power and influence to bully the poor which is how the proverb "wan e jin qian" 万恶金钱 (money is evil) originated. Few adopted the attitude of being indifferent to money and accepting that "qian cai shen wai wu" 钱财身外物 (money and wealth are but material things outside the body of man).

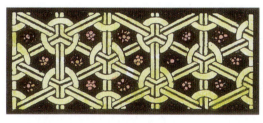

yin ding 银锭 *representing wealth.*

In old China the way inheritances were handed down from one generation to another often created tragic events and the break up of families. During that time only male descendants were entitled to any inheritance. If a man died without a male heir his entire estate would go to his brother's sons instead of to his wife and daughters. Such social practices gave licence to men whose wives had not produced male heirs to be promiscuous and they often had concubines. Even in families with male heirs there were instances of brothers fighting against one another because of inheritance money.

An interesting story was told about a man who protected himself against his children who were selfishly after his money. The man kept a big chest of stones locked up under his bed for years giving the impression to his selfish children that he had gold pieces locked up in the chest. The man's children pretended to be filial towards him and fed him until he died. When the chest was finally opened it was found to be completely filled with stones on which was placed a note which read: "lao zi, lao zi! ruo wu shi zi, e si lao zi" 老子老子 若无石子, 饿死老子。(Old man, old man! If there were no stones old man would have starved to death).

Most modern Chinese are hardworking and thrifty and choose to save a portion of their income for a rainy day. They are very practical and accept that money is a necessary evil and is intended for circulation. They regard it as being as important as food and so their new year greetings to their friends and relatives are centred on the theme of prosperity and wealth.

Gui wen 龟文 *representing longevity.*

1.6 Important events in life

Whenever we met an obstacle in life, my grandfather used to tell us that it was our fate and it would be better that we accepted it and got on with life instead of regretting and brooding over it. He brought his beliefs, religion, practices and values when he came from Guangdong at the age of 16 and, as an overseas Chinese in Malaysia, he adhered to these principles until the day he died. One of his beliefs was that the fate of a child was sealed the moment he was born. His life, his marriage and even his death were predetermined and these events should be observed as important milestones.

In the early 20th century in some parts of China it was of vital importance to observe certain practices in announcing the arrival of the newborn child. If a male was born a bow was hung at the main door but if a female was born a curved tile was displayed. An auspicious name was chosen by the head of the household (the grandfather, and if he had passed away, the father) so that he or she would have a good name to live up to. The baby's head was shaved before the end of the first month so that the baby would have healthy hair. A celebration and feast would be arranged on the day of the full moon and red eggs (symbolising auspicious offspring) and sour ginger pieces (the word for sour sounds like sun 孙 a grandchild, thus a piece of very sour ginger signified a good grandchild) would be distributed to relatives

轩辕黄帝四季诗
生在黄帝头，处世多高位，一世永无忧，君子好筹谋
生在黄帝手，初年平平稳，营谋本钱够，积聚十分有。

Part of the si ji shi 四季诗 which predicts the fate of man based on the birth date with reference to the seasons.

and close friends to signify the auspicious birth of a child to the parents and a filial grandchild to the grandparents.

The practice of breastfeeding a child until he or she is one year old (a one-year-old is regarded as a two-year-old to the Chinese because they include the gestation period) was carried on in my mother's generation. But a working mother today can only afford to breastfeed her child for one or two months, depending on the length of her maternity leave.

Overseas Chinese celebrate their birthdays every year, unlike their forefathers who would normally have their birthdays celebrated by their parents when they turned two years old (Chinese age). After that men (being yang and masculine) would celebrate their birthdays when they reached the Chinese age of 51, 61, 71, 81 and 91 (yang numbers) while women (being yin and feminine) 50, 60, 70, 80 and 90 (all being yin numbers). It was believed that anyone celebrating his birthday before he reached 51 was a pompous person.

Chinese weddings were, and still are very important ceremonies as the Chinese regard marriage as one of the three most important events (the others being birth and death) in a person's life. Ancient rituals of a wedding were attributed to Zhou Gong 周公 a prince during the reign of Zhou Wu Wang 周武王 (1066–1063 BC), who set the six rules in the Book of Rites for the union of a couple. A marriage was to be "mei shuo zhi yan, fu mu zhi ming" 媒妁之言, 父母之命 (listen to the marriage broker and obey the command of the parents). A

young couple did not have to meet and fall in love before they were married because the purpose of a union was to perpetuate the family line. Most importantly the compatibility in terms of the eight characters (the year, month, day and time of birth) of the couple and the family background had to be considered. It was important that such information be gathered by a marriage broker called a mei po and that the dates of birth be assessed by a geomancer. This was part of the first rite while the second rite was the presentation of the girl's name and particulars. If the horoscopes, eight characters and elements of birth of the

Chinese wedding.

couple were compatible they would be blessed with prosperity, posterity and good health, otherwise the couple would be unhappy and struck by ill luck. Once the birthdates were found to be in harmony and suitable and the parents agreed to arrange the marriage the presentation of betrothal gifts would take place. The third and fourth rites would be carried out, during which the parents of the would-be bridegroom would present gifts such as a jade scepter, a hairpin, biscuits, pieces of cloth and tea leaves, which symbolized firm commitment, as a tea plant cannot be transplanted, through the marriage broker. The fifth rite might be carried out after years of engagement and it consisted of the choosing of an auspicious day for the wedding. The sixth rite was the most important as it was the actual wedding and consummation of the marriage. Before the wedding day the exchange of gifts between the two families took place.

The gifts for the bride included red embroidered satin, gold jewelry and money sealed in red packets. The parents of the bride would send her dowry of household utensils, furniture, jewelry and a special item consisting of a bronze bucket and a pair of shoes to symbolise prosperity and harmony for the new couple.

The bride had to perform many ceremonial rites after the wedding dinner, such as walking on sackcloth, covering her head, drinking wine with the groom, sitting in bed and being teased by relatives. These practices are no longer in fashion. After the wedding dinner the married couple retired to their bedroom or went off on honeymoon. By the early 20th century the wedding ceremony had become quite elaborate. The bridegroom sent a sedan chair which arrived at the bride's home accompanied by a group of Chinese musicians sounding gongs and blowing trumpets. The bride, dressed in a classical costume and headdress, had to be carried out to the sedan chair by the marriage broker as she was not to walk on the ground, which was believed to be contaminated by evil spirits. She was to shed tears of sorrow at leaving her parents' home.

On her arrival the bridegroom shot three arrows into the air to rid the area of evil spirits. The bride was then carried into the house where the couple prayed and knelt first before the gods and then before the parents, offering tea and receiving red packets and jewelery. Even the marriage broker received a red packet containing more than one banknote. Chinese always regarded a single item as inauspicious because it symbolises loneliness. Happiness comes in doubles. So the red packet should contain at least two notes. After the tea ceremony the sumptuous wedding dinner was hosted by the parents and the couple retired into their bedroom where a pair of elaborately

jin ding 金锭 *representing gold, an auspicious symbol for festival occasion.*

carved long feng 龙凤 (dragon and phoenix) candles were lit symbolising a good and auspicious union. It was believed that if the candles burnt off at the same time the couple would live to a ripe old age together. Otherwise one of them would die earlier, the long symbolising the male and the feng the female.

These marriage customs were carried out within as well as outside China in early 20th century. Modern weddings based on tradition can be almost as elaborate as these. Many overseas Chinese still follow tradition and choose an auspicious time and day for the wedding, although in the present day context traditional practices have been streamlined. From the day the couple meet and fall in love to the time they decide to get married they may or may not host a dinner for the exchange of engagement rings in the presence of parents and friends.

Weddings of the rich still tend to be very elaborate and pompous but the average wage earner may host a simple wedding dinner or reception. Marriage brokers still operate in some Asian countries, although their role in the marriage is different from what it was in the old days. They work in matchmaking agencies, helping people who encounter difficulties in finding their partner in life or who have little opportunity to meet the right partner. These agencies introduce the couples to each other and they do not normally analyse the suitability of birthdates. Instead they use computers to match those who share the same interests or have similar family backgrounds.

Non-Christian Chinese believe in reincarnation and retribution. Death is merely the end of the yang and the beginning of the yin life. How good and kind one is when living in the yang world will decide how well or how cruelly one is treated in the yin world. Soon after death the soul travels through the Ten Courts of Hell to be judged, and so the death must be mourned in the presence of religious leaders and family members with prayers and offerings made to the yin world rulers for leniency and mercy to afford him a less tortuous journey through the gates of hell. The death ceremony was, and still is, an elaborate and important event to mark the end of life and possibly the beginning of another better life.

Urns containing the ashes of the deceased.

In the early part of the 20th century within, as well as outside China the Chinese bought their own graves long before they were very ill or dying. They would ensure that the feng shui of a site was auspicious by engaging the services of a geomancer. If death occurred unexpectedly the corpse would be stored in a mortuary for months while the family looked for a suitable burial site.

Longevity clothes (the clothes worn for burial) were made as soon as one was seriously ill, or reached the age of 60. Although the traditional longevity clothes are seldom used nowadays, the practice of making up and putting the best dress on the dying is still observed because the Chinese believe that the spirit or ghost will forever appear as he does on his dying day. Sometimes jewelry and favourite objects are buried with the dead and specially printed yin world money is burnt for them because it is believed that such items will be received and used in the other world.

The traditional death rituals are still practised even outside China. Firstly, all mirrors in the hall where the dead is placed have to be covered so that the reflective quality of the mirrors will not adversely affect the dead. A specialist or make-up artist will be engaged to clean the body with water brought in from a nearby stream or source by the eldest son. He or she dresses and makes up the face of the dead who is then laid into the coffin in the presence of the family. The dead lies facing the main door, over which hangs a white banner, to symbolise his willingness to leave the yang world. Offerings are made to the dead and to the deities on the family altar or altars specially set up beside the corpse. The cover of the coffin is fixed until a priest has chosen an auspicious time for the funeral and burial rituals.

Dress codes for the mourning family members are still followed. The closest relatives, the children and their spouses, wear black and sackcloth. The children of brothers and their spouses wear black, the children of sisters, their spouses and other relatives wear blue, and the grandchildren wear white. If the deceased was an old man and his surviving wife was an old lady, she would not have to wear black otherwise she should follow the children and wear black.

Funeral rituals vary depending on whether Buddhist or Daoist priests are engaged for the chanting of prayers. Usually these rituals last for 7 to 49 days depending on how much the family wishes to spend. Relatives and friends pay their last respects by keeping company with the bereaved family members in the evenings and some even throughout the night. Meals and snacks are served in the late evenings.

Outside China, in the Southeast Asian region the burial ceremony for a non-Christian has become less elaborate even though there are still rituals to be followed and the funeral procession can be very long. Some of the rules to be observed may have their origin in superstitious beliefs. For example, special yin world money has to be scattered all the way from the house to the burial ground to pay off wandering souls so that they will not obstruct the way.

When the coffin is nailed down, or lowered into the ground to be buried, the family members are not to look at it or else they will suffer ill luck. Before the coffin is lowered into the grave a cock is thrown across the grave and it must be caught by the eldest son. If he fails to catch the cock bad luck may befall the family. Every member of the family is to throw some earth into the grave and walk off quickly never looking back or else the dead will be unwilling to leave the family behind to proceed to the yin world.

Funeral processions in present day Chinese society are still colourful and often cause traffic jams. A pair of white lanterns carried at the beginning of the procession announce the surname and age of the deceased (the age is equal to the real age plus three, which represents tian or heaven, di or earth and ren or man). Although it was once the practice to have an altar with the spirit tablet and a large photo carried just after the lanterns nowadays these are carried on the carriage (either a lorry or a special vehicle) with the catafalque. The procession that follows consists of musicians and carriers of banners. The carriage of the catafalque is decorated with symbols. For example, if the deceased is a female it is decorated with the colourful mock up of a phoenix. But if the deceased is a male a lion is used to signify his spirit. The bereaved family members follow the carriage on foot for a mile or so and then board the vehicles specially arranged for the purpose.

Chinese cemetery

Once the procession reaches the temple or offertory shrine everyone takes a rest while the family of the deceased make offerings to the deities and have the specially prepared roasted meat, food and drinks distributed to all present. Since funeral rituals are very stressful events pregnant women are advised not to attend. Some even believe that pregnant women who are unlucky may even be harmed by evil spirits causing them to miscarry. Those relatives and friends who have given gifts, condolences, paid tribute to the deceased and spent time with the family during their bereavement will have some meat and food reserved and sent to their homes. After the food has been consumed the acquaintances will leave while the close friends, relatives and family members will proceed to the grave for the burial ceremony. The priests chant prayers before the lowering of the coffin into the grave. Certain practices mentioned earlier such as the throwing of the cock over the grave and the throwing of earth into the grave are then observed. By the time the burial ceremony is over and the family members return to their house it has been given a spring cleaning. The special altar for the deceased is then set up permanently.

On the third day the soul of the deceased is supposed to return to see his family members for the last time. So a table laden with different types of meat, fruits and wine is prepared to welcome the spirit. A pair of large joss sticks and candles are also burnt at the particular time when the soul is supposed to arrive. It is believed that joss sticks send messages to the underworld and candles provides some means of communication. When the soul arrives the candle fire will turn blue and strange things, such as a vision of the soul, may be seen. Dogs may howl and doors may be swept open or shut by the wind. The soul is believed to be assisted in the yin world and consoled by the offerings of prayers at intervals of seven days and finally in the seventh week.

Chinese feast during a traditional funeral ritual.

1.7 | Festivals

The most auspicious time of the year is the first day of the Chinese calendar which all people of the Chinese race call xin nian 新年 (new year). The origins of the new year are shrouded in myth and legend. One source says that it is named after a mythical animal called nian 年. It appears that in ancient China a village was regularly visited by a mythical beast which killed people and devoured domestic animals. It terrorised the villagers so much that they finally united and made an effort to rid themselves of the beast. They gathered with weapons, gongs, fire crackers and red banners. The moment the beast appeared they struck it with their weapons, sounded the gongs to deafen it, let off the fire crackers to frighten it and waved the red banners to distract it. The beast was badly hurt and disappeared forever. The villagers were jubilant and spread the good news to the rest of China. They named that particular day nian and because it happened to be at the end of the winter season and at the beginning of spring it was then called xin nian (new year). Ever since then the Chinese have celebrated this day to mark the beginning of a new period of happiness and goodwill. Chinese all over the world still celebrate the new year according to the lunar calender (so called because it is based on a cycle of the moon, from one new moon to another) although they may also celebrate the English new year according to the Gregorian calendar.

Much preparation is involved in welcoming the Chinese New Year. Weeks ahead, the house is given a spring cleaning with bamboo leaves which sweep away poor luck and window curtains and other household furnishings are washed. New year sweet cakes, biscuits and dried foods are prepared and kept for the celebration. Artists make a special effort to paint nian hua 年画 (new year paintings), while calligraphers write chun lian 春联 (new year poems).

On the 24th day of the 12th lunar month the kitchen god of every house is given offerings of sticky new year cakes and cooked food

A calligrapher writing New Year greetings.

so that he will make a good report on the members of the family as he makes his annual trip to the heavenly gods. Some believe that the sticky nian cakes might seal the lips of the kitchen god so that he cannot utter a word to the heavenly gods about the family's behaviour. New year greeting cards are prepared and sent, and they are usually red to symbolise happiness. This practice started thousands of years ago. During the Western Han era greeting cards were made from bamboo with the name of the sender engraved in the bamboo. By the Song dynasty cards were made from paper. Now greetings cards with good wishes are exchanged.

On the eve of the lunar new year the house is in perfect condition and the people are looking forward to a happy new year. The members of a family gather to share a reunion dinner to signify the unity and love shared between them. The dinner is the most sumptuous of the year and the dishes convey auspicious significance. Food such as chicken meat, abalone, fish, pork, and many varieties of vegetables are the favourite courses. Wine and drinks are also served, usually amidst laughter.

On the eve of the new year even children keep vigil until midnight, as it is believed that, if they do so, their parents will enjoy longevity. This practice may have its origin in the legend of nian, the beast that devoured men in ancient times. People who kept vigil escaped unharmed while those who did not were devoured by the beast. At midnight the housewife prays to the heavenly gods for the blessings of a prosperous and healthy year.

In the old days bamboo was burnt. Later on fire crackers were burnt to welcome the new year. But now in some Southeast Asian countries this practice has been discontinued because of the danger of fire crackers exploding accidentally causing fire or injury. The letting off of fire crackers has its origin in a legend. It seems that a tribe resembling pigmies once lived on Zhongshan. These people were different because each had only one leg. The Chinese were reluctant to associate with them because they carried a virus that caused fever. On the first day of the year they went down the hill to visit friends. To frighten them away people who were prejudiced let off fire crackers.

On the first day of the lunar year everyone wears his or her best clothes. No one is to utter any ill-intentioned word or to break anything or else there will be a separation of family members or ill luck will befall them. Although these beliefs have their origin in superstition a Chinese will not risk ill luck on the very first day of the new year. Instead of feeling lonely and depressed one should be united with one's immediate family members and feel happy because it is believed that the emotions experienced during the fifteen-day new year period will be repeated throughout the year. Thus all debts must be settled before the arrival of the new year and all must wear their best clothes and be in their best spirits. The elders distribute gifts of money sealed in red packets to the young and the unmarried to wish them a good year. In return the young greet their elders and pay their respects, wishing them a happy and healthy year.

On the second day of Chinese New Year a feast of vegetarian food is served to celebrate kai nian 开年 (opening the year). Food and wine are offered to the ancestors. Again the members of the family sit down to share a meal, greeting each other cheerfully. After lunch the family pay visits to senior relatives. This practice is called bai nian 拜年 (paying respect during new year). It is customary for the young to visit their elders and bring oranges to them to wish them a prosperous year. In return the elders give the young unmarried visitors envelopes containing money (between two and ten dollars, or possibly more) for good luck. The guests are served with all sorts of new year biscuits and cakes and there is usually a tray, on which five different types of dried fruits are arranged, including sweet, hot, sour and bitter flavours to symbolise the richness of life. On the third and fourth days the sons-in-law and daughters return to pay their respects and to exchange gifts of Chinese oranges, ji 桔 (ji sounds like luck) which symbolise wealth and fortune. The fifth day is not a popular day for visiting as it is called the po ri 破日 (the broken day). On this day the Chinese pray to the gods of wealth (there are five of them) and welcome them with offerings.

It is believed that the first seven days of the year are dedicated to particular living beings: the first day to chickens; the second to dogs; the third to pigs; the fourth to goats; the fifth to oxen; the sixth to horses and the seventh to

Lion Dance

human beings. Some people paint chickens and hang them up, hoping that by doing so they will be lucky throughout the year. Similarly eating raw fish on the seventh day is symbolic of achieving success, because the fish has always been a symbol of success. In old China the merrymaking and visiting of relatives and friends carries on for 15 days. But although in the present day context most people have to return to work on the third day, the visitation of friends may be continued in the evenings and at weekends. Throughout these fifteen days lion dances are staged to bring good fortune to the business communities. In old China people lit special lights in front of their houses to celebrate the shang deng 上灯 (putting on the light) festival on the fifteenth day. The lights were taken down on the eighteenth day.

On the 106th day after the winter solstice the Chinese pay respect to their deceased

Seasoned food such as waxed ducks for Chinese New Year celebration.

ancestors by visiting and tidying the grave-yards. Offerings of food and wine are made on this day which is the beginning of spring. This practice began at the start of the reign of the first Jin dynasty emperor, Jing Wen Gong 景文公 because he abstained from meat and paid respect to his deceased loyal subject, Jie Zi Tui 介子推 on that particular day. When Wen Gong was a refugee running from the vicious plot of his father's favourite concubine Zi Tui fed the starving Wen Gong with his own flesh. After WenGong had re-established himself and gained the throne he wanted to reward Zi Tui. But Zi Tui wished to be a recluse in a large forest. The anxious emperor thought that he could force Zi Tui out of retirement by setting fire to the forest. Unfortunately Zi Tui lost his way and was burnt to death. Jing Wen Gong was grieved by the event and he mourned the death of Zi Tui. Thus the practice of Qing Ming or all souls day has been carried on until the present day.

On the fifth day of the fifth lunar month the Chinese commemorate the death of Qu Yuan 屈原 (340–278 BC), a patriot and a poet who was a citizen of Chu during the Warring States. Qu Yuan hated the decadence, weakness and corruption of his state, which was attacked by the powerful Qin state. He was so concerned and so frustrated that one day, the fifth day of the fifth lunar month, he threw himself into the lake of Mi Luo Jiang 汨罗江. On seeing him jump from his boat fishermen raced to rescue him, but in vain. In their sorrow they threw their left over food, mainly consisting of glutinous rice, into the lake, so

Lake of Mi Luo Jiang 汨罗江.

that the sea creatures would spare Qu Yuan's body. The story of his death spread. People who admired him commemorated his life by racing dragon boats on the anniversary of his death and this practice has grown into a festival, during which glutinous rice cakes wrapped in bamboo leaves are eaten. The practice of wrapping these cakes with bamboo leaves started during the Han dynasty as it was believed that Qu Yuan appeared in someone's dream and requested that the offering of glutinous rice cakes should be wrapped with bamboo leaves so that the sea creatures could not swallow them.

Another legend associated with this festival relates the story of Cao Er 曹二, a filial daughter of the East Han period. It seems that Cao Er was only fourteen years old when her father was drowned in a lake. She rushed to look for his corpse and searched for it for seventeen days. She then jumped into the lake and, after five days, her spirit appeared, holding her father's body, before the villagers, who were deeply touched by her filial piety and commemorated her death from then on.

In the old days matchmaking was practised not just on earth but also in the heavenly kingdom. It appeared that during the Tang dynasty, on the bank of the westerly river in the heavenly kingdom there lived a good looking and honest cowherd who was noted for his dedication to his job. His industry was made known to the heavenly king who had an equally hardworking daughter who was a marvellously skilful weaver. The king matchmade the couple who fell so deeply in love that they neglected their work. Their behaviour enraged the king who then decided to separate them and sent one off to the eastern and the other to the western side. The loving couple were only allowed to meet once a year, on the seventh day of the seventh lunar month, provided there were enough magpies to form a bridge to link the east to the west. Since then the Chinese have prayed for good weather on this day so that the magpies can gather to form a bridge for the cowherd and the weaver to meet. This offering of prayers and food for a good union is celebrated mostly by maidens as the festival of Qixi 七夕 (seventh night). On the night of Qixi a stage is set with an embroidered picture of the Weaver and the Cowherd. The Weaver is portrayed holding a needle and sewing a garment. On a table are placed plates of fruit and other food with a bowl of water, on which floats a needle specially made for the occasion.

Eight days after the Qixi festival the Chinese observe the Zhong Yuanjie 中元节 or Hungry Ghost festival. It is believed that on that day the god of earth visits the heavens and reports on the good and bad deeds of men. On the same day the hungry ghosts are allowed to leave the gate of hell. These ghosts have to be pacified and so most Chinese families make offerings of joss and yin money to the wandering ghosts. Some Chinese associations set up stages in the compounds of the community halls. A high platform is built displaying icons of the judge of hell and fruit, rice, meat dishes and wine offerings are placed on tables. This festival used to be celebrated with the lighting of paper boats in China, especially in places situated along a riverside. People gathered along the river and let their lighted wooden or paper boats float and drift on the river to guide the souls of those who have drowned in the rivers to a place of rest.

The Zhong Yuanjie is followed by the Zhong Qiujie 中秋节, the moon festival, also known as the lantern festival which is celebrated on the fifteenth day of the eighth lunar month. This festival has its origins in the successful revolution that overthrew the tyrant Yuan ruler. The leader of the revolutionary peasants was Zhu Yuan Zhang 朱元璋 who formed a plan to unite the peasants. On the fifteenth night of the eighth full moon secret messages were hidden in cakes of lotus seed paste which were circulated to the revolutionaries without arousing the suspicion of the

A festive occasion is celebrated with a nine-course dinner at a table covered with a red table cloth.

Yuan soldiers. Zhu Yuan Zhang and his men succeeded in their attempt and overthrew the Yuan to establish the Ming dynasty.

The celebration of the full moon festival has been carried on to the present time. On the night of the moon festival the sky is brightly lit by the full moon and the best way to eat moon cakes is with the family by moonlight. The bright moonlight also reminds its admirers the story of Chang E 嫦娥, the goddess of the moon. She was the wife of Hou Yi 后羿, the best archer in the 3rd century BC. She was believed to have flown off to the moon after she swallowed a pill of immortality which she took from her husband.

On the ninth day of the ninth lunar month the Chinese celebrate the Chongyang festival. It is called Chongyang (double yang) because nine is a yang number (thus the ninth day of the ninth month is double yang). This festival started in the Han dynasty during the reign of Han Gao Zu 汉高祖 (in 200 BC). During this festival people make it a point to climb hills and high land for luck in promotion. They also drink a wine made from chrysanthemums for longevity. Some throw a certain Chinese herb to repel evil influences. Housewives make a special cake with rice and bean flour and a lot of raising agent to symbolise the rise in rank and status.

Presently, the festivals and cultural activities described above are still practised in many parts of China as well as outside China. In spite of changes owing to economical and other forces Chinese culture has remained essential especially to those outside China because it

has become their proud heritage and a way of life deeply embedded in their social organisation.

The ghost slayer, Xhong Kui.

2 Chinese beliefs and practices

晨诣超师院读禅经
chén yì chāo shī yuàn dú chán jīng

前人
qián rén

汲井漱寒齿，　清心拂尘服。
jí jǐng shù hán chǐ,　qīng xīn fú chén fú

闲持贝叶书，　步出东斋读。
xián chí bèi yè shū,　bù chū dōng zhāi dú

真源了无取，　妄迹世所逐。
zhēn yuán liǎo wú qǔ,　wàng jī shì suǒ zhú

遗言冀可冥，　缮性何由熟?
yí yán yì kě míng,　shàn xìng hé yóu shú?

道人庭宇静，　苔色连深竹。
dào rén tíng yǔ jìng,　tái sè lián shēn zhú

日出雾露余，　青松如膏沐。
rì chū wù lù yú,　qīng sōng rú gāo mù

淡然离言说，　悟悦心自足。
dàn rán lí yán shuō,　wù yuè xīn zì zú

This poem by Qian Ren on the morning reading of the Buddhist scripts at the monastery showed clearly how one felt when one entered the monastery with Sutras in one's hand.

CONTENTS

2.1 | Beliefs

In ancient times the Chinese worshipped many gods including natural forces, mythical animals and strange spirits. Paying respect to ancestors started hundreds of years before the birth of Christ and the burial ceremony was formalised before the rule of the first emperor. Articles, utensils and even human lives were offered for the deceased as the Chinese believed that death was an extension of life. At the death of an elder the younger members held mourning and burial rituals for as long as seven weeks. At the end of the burial ceremony a spirit tablet, bearing the dates of birth and death of the deceased and representing the presence of the deceased, would be placed on an altar. It was believed that the deceased could intercede to the gods for his family. Filial piety from the young was demonstrated by offerings of joss, food and wine being placed on the altar. This is still practised by most Chinese families.

By the time of Confucius, in the 6th century BC, primitive religious practices had been modified and Confucianism was officially sanctioned. Confucianism was closely linked with paying respect to ancestors because it taught man to be filial to his elders and to love his fellow men. It was started by Confucius (551–497 BC), an exceptional scholar and philosopher from the state of Lu. He became the Secretary of Justice but when his ideals were not fulfilled he resigned from his post and travelled around, teaching and editing the classics, Shijing 诗经 (a collection of 305 songs and sacred anthems), Liji 礼记 (a record of government systems and rituals of early Zhou dynasty), Shujing 书经 (early historical documents), Chunqiu 春秋 (a chronicle of events from 722 to 481 BC) and Yijing 易经 (a collection of mutations in human events based on the changing arrangements of the eight trigrams). The essence of Confucian teaching is the restoration of a social order and man should value humanity, have benevolence and perfect virtue. Man must possess qualities such as tolerance, reciprocity, courtesy, magnanimity, trust, industry and kindness.

The ancestor A shrine in the Temple of Heavens, Beijing.

During the same period Daoism and Lao Zi's philosophy became popular. Lao Zi 老子 was born in 604 BC in Hunan. He believed that man should live in harmony with nature and that he could do so through dao 道 the way (the natural way in nature). He advocated three "treasures", namely love, frugality and weakness. Daoism was popularised by Zhang in 143 AD as he combined sorcery with the philosophy of the yin/yang school. However, later Lao Zi's followers synthesized his philosophy with other philosophies and finally in the 5th century AD Daoism became an organised religion.

A Shenist medium in a trance.

The features of Daoism were reflected on the altar in a Daoist temple. Stars, ancestors, historical beings and inanimate objects were worshipped. Daoist paradise is known as shoushan 寿山 (the hill of longevity). In Southeast Asian countries there are numerous Daoist temples and places of worship.

A sectarian religion established in the Southeast Asian region that came from China is the True Void Doctrine. It was started by Liao Di Pin 廖帝聘 of Guangxi province. Liao was interested in cults from an early age. He became a disciple of the patriarch Liu Bi Fa at the Yun Gai Dong 云盖峒 monastery and lived an ascetic life for six years. He then returned to his village and preached the True Void Doctrine and helped to cure many of opium addiction.

Buddhism flourished by the end of the Han dynasty. It was based on the teaching of Siddhartha, popularly known as Buddha, the enlightened one who gave up his life of luxury to make sacrifices for his own and man's enlightenment. Buddha, a prince, was born at the foot of the Himalayan Mountains. When he reached the age of 29 he left his home to search for truth and peace. He spent years in self-sacrifice, striving for his enlightenment and practising meditation and self discipline. For 45 years he preached to countless disciples, and then, lying on a couch covered with blossom between two sala trees one day, passed peacefully away. The principles of Buddhism are: not to slay, not to steal, not to be lustful, not to be light in conversation and not to drink wine.

A Chinese Buddhist temple.

During the Tang dynasty Confucianism, Daoism and Buddhism were combined to form the Syncretic Three-in-one Doctrine and this was practised side by side with Ancestor Worship. Syncretism embraces all three basic religions: Buddhism, Daoism and Ancestor Worship. Followers of Syncretism may visit temples devoted to holy spirits and those dedicated to Three-in-One, the Great Way of Former Heaven, the True Void and the Doctrine of Huang. In a temple dedicated to the Three-in-One Doctrine, Confucius is the main object of worship. In temples where the doctrine of the Great Way of Former Heaven, Guan Yin and Confucius are the main deities. Paying respect to deceased ancestors was closely practised with burial rituals which were evident during the rule of Emperor Shi (150 BC). During that time life sacrifices were made as part of burial rituals. It was, and still is, believed that the well being of the dead could affect the fortunes of his descendants and so he must be buried in an auspicious burial ground with good feng shui and offerings of joss and food must be made to demonstrate the filial piety of the descendants.

Overseas Chinese communities still follow these religions and most of them pay respect to deceased ancestors as a sign of filial piety towards their ancestors. Many Chinese especially those overseas have been converted to Christianity which was first brought to China in the 7th century. The belief in Jesus Christ as the saviour of man is now part of Chinese culture which is defined as the total way of life. Culture can be classified in three ways namely the aspect of life related to things, to society and to spiritual life. Religion is certainly an aspect of life related to the spiritual life.

2.2 Chinese deities

Most Chinese pray to as many deities as they can because each deity grants a special favour. Generally Buddhists pay respect to Buddhist deities and Daoists to Daoist deities. The following section describes some of the Chinese deities.

Buddhist deities
AMITABHA (阿弥陀佛)

"Amitabha" means "boundless light" and it is the abbreviated form of "Namah Amitabha", which means "hear us, Amida Buddha!". His image is often seen in the main prayer hall of the Buddhist monastery by the side of Shakyamuni Buddha.

According to the sutra, in the 5th century AD, a monk named Dharmakara made a number of vows, one of which was that if he achieved Buddhahood he would be enlightened if anyone sincerely desired to be born into his Buddha country. Dharmakara became a Buddha and he became Amitabha. Amitabha has many followers in China and the Southeast Asian region where the majority of Buddhists believe that by worshipping him they will be born into the "Pure Land". He is the "Impersonal Buddha" and is said to be at the "Paradise of Pure Land" in which the souls of the pious may rest in peace and happiness.

Amitabha.

ANANDA (阿难)

Ananda, cousin of Shakyamuni Buddha, was one of the principal and favoured disciples of the Buddha. He became a monk in the second year of the Buddha's ministry. Under Buddha's guidance, he developed a very good memory and was famous for the role he performed at the first council for the formation of the Buddhist canon. In the twenty-fifth year of the Buddha's ministry, Ananda became the Buddha's personal attendant and he attained "Enlightenment" and became an Arhat just before the first council was held. According to legend, he lived to the age of 120 years. He is to reappear on earth as a Buddha.

CHENG-HUANG (城隍)

Cheng-huang is the city god. Every city in China used to be fortified by a wall made up of two battlemented walls with earth filling. A ditch is made running parallel to the wall. The Cheng-huang is the spiritual official of the city or town. All the numerous Cheng-huangs constitute a celestial "Ministry of Justice", presided over by a Cheng-huang-in-chief.

Emperor Yao (2357 BC) instituted a sacrifice called *ba jie* in honour of the Eight Spirits and one of them was the Cheng-huang. Hence people began to pray to the city god for peace, prosperity and good health. During the early Ming period, the addresses and the official titles of the city god were regulated. In the capital, he was called "Di" (帝), at large cities he was named "Wang" (王), in towns he was called "Gong" (公), and in smaller towns he

Cheng Huang, the city god.

was known as "Hou" (侯).

The temples for the worship of the Cheng-huang in ancient China looked like the official buildings of the governing authority and the ranking of the city god followed closely the official status of the governing official.

A temple caretaker explains that the city god is just like a civil servant to the "Heavenly Supreme". In ancient China, a public service-man well-known for his efficiency and good deeds could be canonised after his death to be the city god of the village or town where he used to serve.

DIAMOND KINGS OF HEAVEN (四大金刚)

The four great Diamond Kings are the Heavenly Guardians or *Devas*. They are governors of the continents lying at the four cardinal points from Mount Sumeru which is believed by the Buddhists to be the centre of the world. They are supposed to bestow happiness on those who respect the "Three Buddhist Treasures" — the Buddha, the Law, and the Priesthood.

Mo-li Qing (魔礼青), the eldest, is eight metres tall. He has a fair complexion but a ferocious look. He carries a magic jade ring and a spear with a magic sword, on which are engraved the Chinese characters of Earth, Water, Fire and Wind. When used, it creates strong winds which produce tens of thousands of spears that pierce the bodies of enemies and turn them to dust. The wind would be followed by fire, which would create tens of thousands of poisonous serpents. A thick smoke would then rise out of the ground, blinding and killing all enemies.

Mo-li Hong (魔礼红) carries in his hand an "Umbrella of Chaos", made of beautiful pearls. When he opens it, all the heavens and earth will be covered with darkness. When he turns it upside down, it creates terrific storms in the sea and violent earthquakes on earth.

Mo-li Hai (魔礼海) holds a four-stringed guitar, which supernaturally affects the earth, water, fire or wind. When it is played, the camps of the enemies will perish in fire.

Mo-li Shou (魔礼寿) has two whips and a bag which keeps a certain creature which assumes the form of a white, winged elephant and devours all enemies on command.

The worship of the four Diamond Kings was started by Bu Kong (不空), a Singhalese Buddhist in the 8th century (AD).

He advocated that the four Diamond Kings were stationed at the four corners of the world. They were the protectors of the centre of the universe and the home of the gods. They were mentioned in the Buddhist scriptures as being the guardians of the four doors of the hall where Buddha played with the twenty-four *Devas*.

Their images or statues were first popularised by the Tang Emperor, Xuan Zong (712–756) who ordered their statues placed at the northwest corners of the city to guard against attackers.

GUAN YIN (观音)

Guan Yin, the Goddess of Mercy, was first introduced in the 5th century AD by Gautama Buddha in his preachings. Giles' *Glossary of Reference* has the following description of her: "Sanskrit, Padma-pani, or 'Born of the Lotus'. Her Chinese title signifies, 'she who always observes or pays attention to sounds,' i.e. 'she who hears prayers' ". Also known as the Great Mercy or Great Pity, she is supposed to have a thousand arms and a thousand eyes. She is sometimes addressed as the "Goddess of the Southern Sea" (南海菩萨). The catalogue of the Collection of Chinese Exhibits at the Louisiana Purchase Exposition, St. Louis, 1904, p. 269, has the following report on Guan Yin:

"Her name was Miao Shan, and she was the daughter of an Indian Prince. In order to convert her blind father to Buddhism she transfigured herself as a stranger, and informed him that were he to swallow an eyeball of one of his children, his sight would be restored. But his children would not consent to the sacrifice, whereupon Guan Yin created an eye which her parent swallowed and he regained his sight."

Williams in *The Outlines of Chinese Symbolism and Art Motives* says that the island of Putuo (普陀山), in the Zhoushan Archipelago, is sacred to the Buddhists, the worship of Guan Yin being its prominent feature on account of the fact that the Goddess is said to have resided there for nine years.

Tredwell, in his *Chinese Art Motives Interpreted*, 1915, pp. 83–85, gives the following description of Guan Yin:

"The most unusual and popular representation of this Goddess is a beautiful and gracious woman, who holds a child in her arms and wears a rosary around her neck".

According to one legend, she is said to be the daugher of a ruler of the Zhou dynasty who strongly objected to her becoming a nun. He put her to humiliating tasks in the convent. When his efforts failed, her father ordered her to be executed for disobedience to his wishes. But the executioner felt sorry for Guan Yin and brought it about that the sword which was to descend upon her broke into a thousand pieces. Her father thereupon ordered her to be stifled. Guan Yin died and on her arrival to hell, the flames of fire burst into bloom. So Yama, the presiding officer, sent her back to life again. Carried by a lotus flower, she went to the island of Potala, near Ningpo. One day, Guan Yin's father fell ill. A cure was effected by Guan Yin and in gratitude her father ordered her statue to be made.

KSHITIGARBHA BUDDHA (地藏王)

The Buddha is the guardian of the earth. He possesses powers over the ten courts of hell and devoted his life to the sufferings of all things between Nibbana of Shakyamuni Buddha and the period of the Maitreya Buddha. He is compassionate and is believed to be the deliverer of souls from hell. Legend has it that he once made a strong vow that he will never aim for Buddhahood until he succeeds in leading all devils from their hells to heaven. Thus he is regarded as the redeemer who opens the gates of hell for the suffering souls. He is often seen holding a staff, riding on a chimera, a mythical creature with the head of a lion, the body of a goat and the tail of a dragon, vomiting flames.

MAITREYA BUDDHA (弥勒佛)

The Maitreya is also known as the Coming Messiah or Buddha and the word "Maitreya" means "gentleness". He is always portrayed as a stout and laughing Buddha. He is a Bodhisattva and the successor of Shakyamuni. It is said that Shakyamuni met him at the Fushita heaven and appointed him as his successor to appear as Buddha after the lapse of five thousand years.

Maitreya is worshipped in most of the Chinese Buddhist temples in China as well as in Malaysia and Singapore. His birthday falls

Buddhist deities.

on the auspicious Chinese New Year Day. For this reason, he is also recognised as the Buddha of Happiness.

Daoist deities
YU HUANG (玉皇)

Yu Huang is also known as Shangdi (上帝). Legend has it that the Emperor Zhen Zong (真宗) of the Song dynasty (AD 1005) was forced to sign a peace treaty with the Tungueses. The dynasty was in danger of losing the faith and support of the people. In order to pacify his people the Emperor pretended he was in direct communication with the gods of heaven. One day, he summoned his ministers in the 10th lunar month in 1012, and announced to them, "an immortal brought me a letter from Yu Huang in my dream and told me my ancestor will be sent in person." To his surprise, what he said came true — his ancestor, Tai Zu (太祖), the founder of the dynasty, appeared before him! From that time, the Emperor worshipped Yu Huang.

THE QUEEN OF HEAVEN (天后娘娘)

The Queen of Heaven is a Water Spirit. She has many titles, such as the Queen of Heaven, the Holy Mother (圣母), Lady-in-waiting to Heaven (天妃), Lady-in-waiting to the Sages (天后).

The story about her life is interesting as she is said to have been a virgin named Lin (林), who lived some centuries ago near Foochow. The Chinese encyclopaedia gives an account of her origin. According to this source, the Queen of Heaven was born the sixth daughter of a Fujian sailor named Lin Yuan in the Song dynasty (AD 960–1278). One day, she had a dream in which she saw her father's junk sinking during a storm. She changed into a water spirit and went to his rescue. She died at the early age of twenty, but her spirit had been seen again and again by sailors. During the reign of Emperor Yong Lo of the Ming dynasty (AD 1403–1426) she was deified as Tian Fei (Lady-in-waiting to Heaven), and soon after that a temple was built in her honour.

THE EIGHT IMMORTALS (八仙)

Stories about the Eight Immortals as extraordinary individuals of immortality flourished in the Tang and Song dynasties, but they were

Queen of Heaven.

not grouped together until the Yuan period (AD 1280–1368). The Immortals are Daoist holy spirits. *Shen* or holy spirits were first known during the Warring States period (476–221 BC) with the teachings of Lao Zi (老子) and Zhuang Zi (庄子), the great Daoist philosophers. Very ancient writings, such as the *Li Huo Lun* (理惑论), written by Mou Rong (牟融) of the Eastern Han Dynasty, contain references to spirits or immortals. Du Fu (杜甫) of the Tang Dynasty had written a poem called "The Eight Immortals of the Wine Cup". There are many other accounts of the existence of immortals but the Eight Immortals are much appreciated as religious statues for homes and temples as their portraits and carvings are symbolic of luck and longevity.

GOD OF LITERATURE (文昌)

The God of Literature is a Daoist deity. According to legend, he lived in Sichuan during the Tang dynasty, was reincarnated many times, and was finally deified in the Yuan period, AD 1314. Sometimes he is known as Wen Chang Di Jun (文昌帝君). Devotees worshipped him on the third and eighth moons with sacrifices. He is reputed to be residing in the constellation, Ursa Major, known by the Chinese as Kui (魁), and is said to have transformed himself 99 times.

According to C.A.S. Williams in *Outlines of Chinese Symbolism and Art Motives*, Japan, 1974 — "this powerful divinity is generally represented holding a pen and a book on which is written four characters, meaning 'Heaven decides literary success' ". Sometimes he is portrayed standing with one foot on the head of a large fish, with the other foot lifted. In one hand, he holds a large brush and in the other a cap. The significance of the God standing on the fish is that the carps of the Yellow River are believed to swim up the stream in the third moon of each year, and those which succeed in passing the rapids of "the dragon door" in Hunan immediately change into "dragon fish". This indicates that success and fame will be the rewards of the industrious.

THE GOD OF LONGEVITY (寿公)

The God of Longevity, Shou Xing (寿星), is a stellar deity. Once upon a time, it came down to earth and took a human form. It was said to be a constellation formed of the two star-groups, Jiao and Kang, the first two on the list of twenty-eight constellations. Whenever it appeared in the sky, China enjoyed peace and happiness. When it disappeared, the nation suffered poverty and wars. Qin Shi Huang Di, the first Emperor, was the first to recognise it and offered sacrifices to the star in 246 BC.

The deity is a domestic god with a happy expression and a large forehead. He is portrayed on a stag, holding a large peach, with a flying bat above his head. The stag and the bat both indicate *fu* (福) or happiness. The peach and gourd symbolise longevity.

THE GOD OF WEALTH (财神)

The God of Wealth is a deity to the Chinese. Legend has it that Jiang Zi Ya was at war with

Wu Wang of the Zhou dynasty against the last of the Shang emperors, Zhou Gong Ming, who was an excellent warrior. It appeared that Jiang Zi Ya made a straw image of him, wrote his name on it, burnt incense and chanted prayers for twenty days. On the twenty-first day, some arrows were shot into the eyes and heart of the straw image. At that same moment, Gong Ming felt very ill, and died. Later on he was canonised as the President of Wealth. He is also known as the Star God of Affluence.

Syncretic deities
GUAN DI (关帝), THE GOD OF WAR

Guan Di or Guan Yu was an outstanding patriot and he was a hero of China during the period of the Three Kingdoms (3rd century AD). He was killed by his adversaries led by Sun Quan in AD 219, was canonised nine hundred years later by the Song Emperor (AD 1120) and finally in 1594 was proclaimed a god. The story of Guan Di is as follows:

He left his native Shanxi in search of adventure and on his way, he met an old man who was forced to offer his granddaughter to a government official to be a concubine. Feeling sorry for the man, Guan Yu killed the evil officer. He became a wanted killer and he ran away to Tong Guan Pass — the border between the provinces — but found out that troops of soldiers were looking for him. Feeling dejected, he went to a stream to quench his thirst but to his surprise he realised that his face was transformed from white to red, and thus he was disguised and could slip away from the soldiers. He then met Liu Bei (刘备) and Zhang Fei (张飞) who shared common ideas and aspirations with him. They became blood brothers or sworn-brothers and later they made history in ancient China as war heroes. Legends and stories about miracles accredited to Guan Di even long after his death multiplied and his believers attributed their good fortunes to him. His birthday is now celebrated annually on the thirteenth day of the fifth lunar month. He is also commemorated on the fifteenth day of the second moon. Often portrayed as a warrior riding on a horse, he is shown holding a huge weapon called *guan dao* (关刀).

THE MONKEY GOD (齐天大圣)

The Monkey God is a popular Chinese temple deity in China as well as in Singapore and Malaysia. The *Record of Travels in the West* relates the story of the Monkey God in forty-one chapters but the most commonly read is that written by Wu Cheng En (1500–1582) during the Ming dynasty. The story is supposed to be based on actual historical events that took place during the pilgrimage to India in search of Buddhist scriptures by a priest called Xuan Zang or San Zang during the Tang dynasty (7th century AD).

The opening chapter of the book relates the birth of the Monkey God as follows: "Beyond the seas, there was a famous mountain standing in the kingdom of Peng Lai, known as Hua Guo Shan (花果山). At the top of this mountain there was a huge rock. Since the creation of the Universe, it had been worked upon by the elements. One day it suddenly split open and gave birth to a strange stone about the size of a ball. Fructified by the wind, it assumed the shape of a stone monkey, complete with five senses and four limbs. In no time, the monkey learned to climb and run and he saluted the four quarters."

One version says that the Monkey God started life as a stone that was hatched from a mountain. Through chance he acquired intelligence and immortality.

Another book called *San Zang Qu Jing* (三藏取经) relates that the Monkey God was entrusted to look after the welfare of the Buddhist priest, San Zang, during his journey to the west. Throughout the long, hazardous journey, the Monkey God had to fight against evil spirits and vicious people. Thus he was given the title of "Buddha Victorious Strife".

Another source says that the Monkey God was proclaimed "King of all the Monkeys", under the title, "Handsome Monkey King". He was interested in trying to solve the mysteries of life. After travelling for eighteen years by land and sea, he became the disciple of the "Buddhist Patriarch". His master gave him the name which meant "Obedient and Aware-of-the-Void" (孙悟空). He was able to somersault a distance of nine thousand kilometres and change into seventy-two different forms. He was granted the title of "Heavenly Groom" by the Jade Emperor and later was called "the great sage of all the heavens" (齐天大圣). His feast days are celebrated on the eighteenth day of the fifth moon and on the eighteenth day of the eighth moon.

NE ZHA (哪吒)

Ne Zha (The Third Prince) is portrayed in China as well as in Singapore as holding his magic bracelet in one hand and a magic sword in the other, with the "wheels of wind and fire" under his feet. The Third Prince's miraculous birth is recorded in Chapter Twelve of the Chinese version of the *Legends of the Gods* in the following words:

"General Li Jing's wife was Madam Yen. She had already borne him two sons: the eldest was Jin Zha, and the second Mu Zha. Madam Yen carried her third child for three-and-a-half years.

"One night, Madam Yen had a dream in which a Daoist priest went into her bedroom and told her that she would beget the son of the unicorn. She woke up in a fright and she later gave birth to Ne Zha. At the age of seven, the Third Prince was already two metres tall. One day, he accidentally killed the third son of the Dragon King of the Eastern Seas, for which his parents were held responsible. The Third Prince, in order to save his parents from blame, surrendered himself to the Dragon King, and paid for his crimes by scraping the flesh off his bones. His soul returned to the Cavern of the Great Monad and took shelter from his master. His mother built a temple in his honour on the Kingfisher Screen Mountain. Devotees' prayers were answered and the temple became a popular place of worship.

"His master recreated a new Third Prince from water-lily stalks and lotus leaves, and

44

armed him with a fiery spear and a pair of 'wind-and-fire wheels' under his feet".

The birthday of the Third Prince is celebrated annually in great style on the eighth and ninth days of the fourth moon.

GOD OF CARPENTERS (鲁班)

The God of Carpenters used to be called Lu Ban Gong (鲁班公). He was born during the "Spring and Autumn Period". His other name was Gong Shu Zi (公输子). He had exceptional mental faculties and intelligence so people paid tribute to him and named him "the good virtuous and foremost teacher". He was gifted at carpentry. Once he carved a bird out of wood. It became so realistic that it flew away. Most carpenters in China and other Buddhist areas pray to him for guidance.

THE DOOR GODS (门神)

Legend relates that in ancient times, there grew on Mount Du Shu, in the Eastern Sea, an enormous peach tree, the branches of which covered an area of several thousand square kilometres. The lowest branches, which inclined towards the northeast, formed the "Door of the Devils", through which millions of devils passed in and out. Two spirits, Shen Tu (神荼) and Yu Lei (郁垒), were given the task to guard this passage. Those who had been wicked were immediately bound by them and delivered to be eaten by tigers. When Emperor Huang heard of this he had the portraits of the two spirits painted on peachwood tablets and hung above the doors to keep off evil spirits.

Gradually, people formed the habit of painting the portraits of the Door Gods and had them pasted on the doors, showing Shen Tu and Yu Lei armed with bows, arrows and spears.

In later times, the Door Gods were made even more popular by the ministers of the Emperor Tai Zong (太宗) of the Tang dynasty, Qin Shu Bao (秦叔宝) and Fu Jing De (傅敬德).

When Tai Zong was very ill and in a delirium, he heard demons rampaging in his bedroom. The Empress summoned many court physicians for consultation while Qin Shu-bao and Hu Jing-de were assigned to look after the Emperor. They stood guard dressed like the Door Gods outside the palace gate all night, while the Emperor slept in peace. When the Emperor recovered from his illness, people believed that the Door Gods had kept the evil spirits away.

THE KITCHEN GOD (灶君)

According to the legends, the Kitchen God or the God of the Stove met a Daoist priest of the Qi State who obtained from him the secrets of immortality. The priest then went to the Emperor Xiao Wu (140–86 BC) of the Han dynasty and told him that he would possess the powers of the God provided that he would agree to patronize and pray to the Kitchen God. The Emperor did and obtained his knowledge of alchemy, which enabled him to make gold in 133 BC.

It seems that the Kitchen God has the power over the fate of the members of each family.

He distributes riches and poverty to people with discretion and makes an annual report to the "Supreme Being" on the conduct of the family on the twenty-third day of the twelfth moon and returns on the thirtieth of the month.

Ceremonies are performed by Chinese seeing him off to Heaven and welcoming him back. He has not been painted so far. His name is usually written in gold letters on a red wooden board for the purpose of worship.

2.3 | Myths

Legend has it that before the world existed the universe was a huge egg-like thing within which Pangu 盘古, a mythical being, lived. After a period of 1800 years the egg-like thing broke up into the heavens and the earth because of the infusion and combination of the yin and yang elements of the egg-shaped thing. Pangu grew a metre a day until he was almost 2 million metres tall! Finally Pangu grew so old that he died giving off his breath as wind and cloud, his blood as river and stream, his scream as thunder and lightning, his eyes as the sun and the moon, his nose and ears as hills and mountains, his bones as minerals and precious stones and his sweat as rain. This story may seem far fetched but another myth is even more fantastic.

This second story believed by the ancients was about Nu Wa 女娲, a lady with a snake's body. She was able to change herself into 70 forms at will. It was said that she created living creatures including man! The mythical Nu Wa had the ability to control the elements. It was rumoured that once the structure that supported the heavens over the earth collapsed and it was she who mended the hole in the structure, preventing the heavens from falling in and destroying the earth.

The most powerful of the mythical beings was perhaps the dragon. The dragon was believed to exist in the swirl of the destructive storm, in flashes and forks of lightning and on mysterious mountain tops. It was considered an auspicious animal even though its foetus was a snake, which, because it took thousands of

Nu Wa 女娲.

years to hatch, was said to have magical powers. There were three species of dragon; the long 龙, the li 蛎 and the jiao 蛟. The long, used as a symbol of power embroidered on garments of the emperors in old China, was scaly and had the head of a camel, the belly of a frog and the claws of a hawk. In the Yijing 易经, a Confucius classic, Fuxi 伏羲, the legendary ruler was said to have changed himself into a dragon when he lived as a hermit under the sea. Thus, emperors of China were said to be sons of the dragon and they alone were fit to wear a yellow robe with the dragon imprint. Their thrones, flags, chariots and palaces were decorated with images of the dragon as symbols of supreme power.

The phoenix was a chimerical creature but it represented the yin power of the empresses of old China. It had the head of a pheasant, the beak of a swallow, the neck of a tortoise and its feathers were multi-coloured. It was a symbol embroidered on all garments and hats worn by the empresses. It lived in China and it appeared only during peacetime. Many legends surround the emperors and warriors.

The most fantastic tales were about Jiang Zi Ya 姜子牙 a general who helped Wu Wang 武王 overthrow the tyrant Zhou Wang 纣王. The fierce battle supposedly fought at Muya 牧野 in 1122 BC became the theme of many fictional tales which are still read today. Jiang Zi Ya and his warriors fought bravely and won, in spite of the intrigues and traps set by Zhou Wang and his aids. Numerous heroes such as Ne Zha 哪吒, Mu Zha 木吒, and others who performed unbelievable feats and had supernatural powers were described in the novel Feng Shen Bang 封神榜.

Closely connected with the burial ritual is the myth of the courts of hell and reincarnation. In the heavens it is believed that there are hundreds of deities but in hell there are ten gates through which every soul has to be judged before he is reincarnated. How did this belief originate? It appears that during the Ming dynasty a governor wandered into hell and discovered it to be a huge landscaped space. He went into the first gate and met Guan Yu 关羽, a Three Kingdoms hero. When he returned he told everyone about his adventure. It was believed that gamblers were punished as soon as they had passed the first gate and were found guilty. Law offenders were beaten, stripped and tortured. In the third week the soul arrived at the mirror of retribution which reflected its past. The good would be rewarded while the bad punished. By the sixth week the soul arrived at the Naihe 奈河 bridge which the wicked would find tortuous to cross. In the seventh week the 10th court of hell would be reached. This court was presided over by Zhuan Lun Wang 转轮王 who would recount the entire past of the soul and list all his good and bad deeds. A judgement would be passed as whether the soul would be reincarnated as a human. Once the decision was made the soul would be sent to Mengpo 孟婆 who would offer a cup of tea to the soul to erase all his memories. The soul would then be driven into the wheel of law and would be reincarnated. This procedure of reincarnation sounds unbelievable but such is the myth that has been created over thousands of years. How many overseas Chinese still believe this today is not known.

2.4 | Martial arts and weapons

Chinese martial arts were created by various families or clans as special ways of training the body and mind and have been practised for thousands of years for self defence and as physical exercise. By the Han dynasty all sorts of sword play was practised by martial artists. During the Sui and Tang dynasties the staging of public martial arts competitions was a means of recruiting warriors: the winners were offered positions in the military service. Towards the end of the Sui dynasty one of the Buddhist monasteries, Shao Lin Si 少林寺 became a well-known centre of martial arts for Buddhist monks. The experts in the temple numbered over 2,000. In the Tang period even poets such as Li Bai 李白 and Du Fu 杜甫 were trained in martial skills. During the Song dynasty all forms of weapons were made for martial training. But during the Yuan dynasty the ruler discouraged the people from using weapons in case they should stage a rebellion. However, the development of martial skills flourished once more during the Ming dynasty. The emperor, Ming Tai Zu 明太祖, himself trained in martial arts and was a great warrior.

Martial artists were very active during the Qing dynasty. Shaolin Quan 少林拳, created at the Buddhist monastery, Shaolin Si 少林寺, at the foot hills Wuru Feng 五乳峰 in Henen in 495 AD, was most popular in the northern region of China. Other martial styles such as Taiji Quan 太极拳, Nan Quan 南拳 and Bagua Quan 八卦拳 also flourished. By the beginning of the era of the Nationalists in 1910 the establishment of Jingwu School of Physical Training 精武体操馆 gave the young the opportunity to train not just in martial arts but also in other western forms of physical training. Presently, Jingwu is found in many parts of the world and the various Chinese martial arts are popular forms of physical training.

There are three basic types of martial art. The first is a form of physical training using various parts of the body to perform the exercises. The second concentrates on martial

A Chinese martial artist.

procedure and includes the use of weapons and the exercise of the body. Taiji Quan, Nan Quan, and Bagua Quan are examples of this. The third type focuses on combat and the training requires at least two people.

The main aim of martial arts training is to instil in the learner a keen sense of alertness and agility, and to develop a strong body which has a powerful flow of qi and vivid spirit. Martial arts certainly enables the practitioner to defend himself effectively. Taiji Quan was created by a Song dynasty martial artist, Zhang San Feng 张三丰, as a form of martial art. Today it is practised as a form of exercise. It is practised under various schools, namely the yangjia 杨家, the chenjia 陈家, the wujia 吴家, and the sunjia 孙家. The basic steps and principles of the various schools of taiji such as peng 棚, ji 挤, an 按, and cai 采 are all similar but the style and speed of movement varies to some degree.

All forms of taiji are based on the activation of qi 气 (energy) in the body through slow and balanced movements as well as the concentration of the mind and spirit to synchronise breathing and movement. Through the exercises the internal organs and the external physical form are energised. The essence of the art of taiji is centred on balance, internal strength, peace of mind and control. Thus for the art to be truly effective on the improvement of health it must be practised slowly, gracefully and correctly every day.

Another form of activating the qi or energy of the body is through training in qigong 气功. This form of martial training is achieved through the art of controlling breathing and

Taiji Quan
Tai 太 means greatest and ji 极 supreme. The Taiji movements of yin (retreat) and yang (forward) always move toward and become each other.

using the willpower to activate the qi as the Chinese say: yi yi yong qi 以意用气. Qigong invigorates the inner energy to improve the function of the nervous system and to strengthen the internal organs.

There are a few schools for the training of qigong. One school teaches the student to mediate and activate the dan tian 丹田, the area 3″ below the navel which is the centre of gravity on the body. Taiji qigong is sometimes called the wu qin qigong 五禽气功. This form is active as the martial artist imitates the movements of either the tiger, deer, bear or crane.

There are 18 types of weapons popularly used by martial artists. They are: gang bian 钢鞭, gong jian 弓箭, chang qiang 长枪, chang mao 长矛, ban fu 板斧, shuang jian 双锏, bi wo 笔挝, sheng suo 绳索, dun pai 盾牌, nu 弩, da dao 大刀, jian 剑, yue 钺, ji 戟, shu 殳, cha 叉, pa 耙, and bai da 白打. Some weapons were favourites of renowned heroes and warriors. For example, the da dao was made in a special way with a long handle for Guan Yu, a loyal subject of Liu Bei 刘备, a warlord of the Three Kingdoms period. Over 2,000 years ago the jian was made famous by the great archer, Hou Yi 后羿, who was believed to have shot down 9 of the mythical 10 suns that almost set the whole earth on fire. The shu and the pa were described in the story of the journey to the west as used by Tang San Zang 唐三藏, the Buddhist patriarch who travelled west to obtain the Buddhist scripts. The other weapons have been used by numerous martial experts throughout history.

Dun pai 盾牌.

There are many types of qigong exercise. Some are like mediation for activating the qi at the dan tian 丹田 of the navel. The technique of activating the qi is through relaxing the body and mind using the will to move the qi.

2.5 | Shu — the five skilful methods

The Chinese method of divination, learnt from their forefathers, concerning guidance for the present and for the future are unique and fascinating. These methods are commonly known as wu shu 武术 (five skilful methods) and they are grouped under shan 山 (the art of building up a vital body and spirit), yi 医 (the art of healing), ming 命 (the art of assessing the date of birth and astrology), bu 卜 (the art of fortune telling) and xiang 相 (the art of face reading, kan yu and selecting auspicious times).

Shan is an abstract term for the art of improving the physical as well as the spiritual health through the appropriate use of medicated wine and herbs. It also includes the study of ancient philosophy and the classics, and training in martial arts. Yi or medical cure is

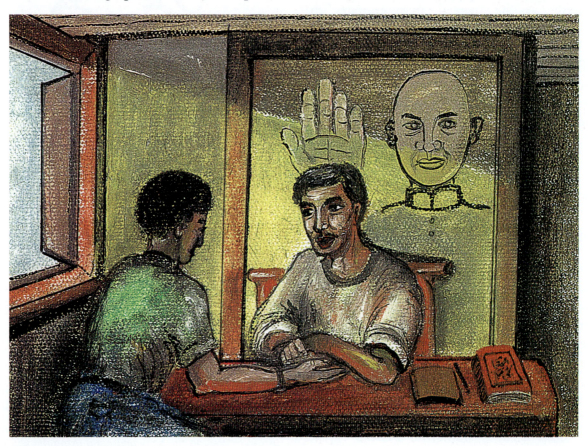

A face and palm reader.

approached in various ways including acupuncture, herbal cures and spiritual cures. Ming or fate represents the skill of assessing the fate of a person based on his date and time of birth. Bu is the art of fortune telling referring to numerology, the hexagrams and other ancient beliefs.

Numerology has always been an important consideration to the Chinese. When a Chinese buys a house or a car he makes sure its number is auspicious, because an auspicious number is believed to bring good fortune and an inauspicious number ill luck.

Some numbers are more significant than others and some combine harmoniously with others while causing disharmony when used with some other numbers. Odd numbers (1,3,5,7,9) are yang while even (2,4,6,8) yin. When a yin number is combined with a yang number it forms a balanced number pair.

The number 3 is significant since there are three important stages in a man's life (his birth, his marriage and his death). But the sound of a number is also important. For example, the number 4 is inauspicious because it sounds like "si" 死 (die), while 8, which sounds like "fa" 发 (luck), and 9, which sounds like "jiu" 久 (longevity), are lucky.

Yi 一 (1) is a yang number representing the direction north and the water element. Er 二 (2) is a yin number symbolising the fire element, the south and the two complimentary forces, yin and yang. San 三 (3) is a yang number categorised with wood and the east. It sounds like "sheng" 生 (growth), and therefore is a popular number. As mentioned earlier, si 四 (4) sounds like si 死 (die) in Cantonese and is avoided. Wu 五 (5) is a yang and lucky number and it has been used to classify many aspects of Chinese things such as the elements, the senses and the basic colours. Liu 六 (6) is a yin number symbolising the element water, and the north. Qi 七 (7) is a yang number and it sounds like "shi" 实 (sure) in Cantonese. It is related to the five element and the south. Ba 八 (8) symbolises the element wood, east and it sounds like "fa" 发 (luck). Jiu 九 (9) symbolises longevity, the element metal and west. Shi 十 (10) is a yin number. (For more information on numbers see Lip: 92).

Xiang is reading the written words, the names, the faces and the kan yu or feng shui of a person. Each skill or knowledge classified under the method or shu is an unique and complicated study.* Shan and yi are introduced in this chapter and kan yu or feng shui, house reading, is elaborated on in Section 3.

The skills of shan and yi have their origin as far back as the 5th century BC, during the Zhou dynasty. Even at that time there were specialists of food and herbal medicine. These specialists were called shiyi 食医 (doctors of food). The shiyi served the first emperor, Qin Shi Huang Di 秦始皇帝, as food advisers. A strategist, Zhou Yi 周易, once said, "Shen yan yu, jie yin shi 慎言语, 节饮食 (be careful with words, stringent on food)" What he meant was that one had to be careful about what one ate

---

*It is not within the scope of this book to elaborate on all of them but the reader may refer to *Chinese Geomancy, Feng Shui for the Home, Feng Shui for Business, Choosing Auspicious Chinese Names, The Chinese Art of Face Reading*, and *Chinese Numbers* for further study.

Qin Shi Huang Di 秦始皇帝.

because if one should eat the wrong food one's health could be affected. The oldest medical text book, called Huang Di Nei Jing 黄帝内经 (the private records for the emperor), was written during the time of the Warring States. It stressed the need to restrain the consumption of food bad for the body and the need to use proper food to nourish the body. An excellent book on food therapy and medicated herbs called Shen Yi Ben Cao Jing 神农本草经 was produced in the Han dynasty, classifying 365 types of herbs. During that era the most noted herbist was Zhang Zhong Jing 张仲景. He used ginger and other herbs to treat the sick. Sun Si Miao 孙思邈 wrote Qian Jin Yi Fang 千金翼方 (A Thousand Ways of Curing) in

the Tang dynasty. More knowledge was gained and more books were published during the Song, Jin and Yuan periods. By the Ming dynasty Chinese herbs were popularly and commonly used. A noted herbist, Li Shi Zhen 李时珍 compiled a book called Ben Cao Gang Mu 本草纲目 over a period of 27 years. This book contained 50 chapters describing over 1800 types of herbs for curing illnesses. This book has survived the test of time and is still being used. The Chinese method of using herbs and food to heal is based on their knowledge on the balance of the yin and yang qualities of herbs and food. They also know that everything can be classified under the 5 elements, Gold, Wood, Water, Fire and Earth. The harmony of the yin and yang and the elements result in equilibrium and well being of the body in physical as well as in spiritual (the qi of the body) forms. They know that an ailment may be external, internal or both. The external causes of illness are physical forces such as climatic and environmental factors including feng shui. The internal causes are more difficult to detect because they are related to the emotions of the affected. Therefore, a Chinese doctor needs to touch, to examine and to speak to the sick in order to diagnose an illness. The patient's body system may be affected by disharmony caused by grief, fear, stress, an unbalanced diet or other undesirable factors.

3 |  Kan Yu, the Chinese art of siting and design

清明

qīng míng

杜 牧
dù mù

清	明	时	节	雨	纷	纷。
qīng	míng	shí	jié	yǔ	fēn	fēn

路	上	行	人	欲	断	魂。
lù	shàng	xíng	rén	yù	duàn	hún

借	问	酒	家	何	处	有?
jiè	wèn	jiǔ	jiā	hé	chù	yǒu

牧	童	遥	指	杏	花	村。
mù	tóng	yáo	zhǐ	xìng	huā	cūn

The proper burial of the ancestors is important in feng shui belief. This poem by Du Mu presents the sad and dismal season of Qing Ming during ancestor worship in the graveyard: "The rain keeps on fallin on the Qing Ming season. . ."

CONTENTS

3.1 | Introduction

Since Kan Yu 堪輿 also known as feng shui 风水 was first practised in China a few thousand years ago, it has been incorporated into Chinese traditional architecture. It became so deeply rooted that the principles and rudiments of building such as symmetry, balance, hierarchy of height, wall-enclosures and orientation were based on its concepts. A 3rd century Chinese dictionary records the choosing of auspicious sites for building purposes, while the Shujing (the Book of Documents) and the Shijing (the Book of Songs), dating back to the Zhou dynasty, contain evidence of the selection of auspicious sites for new capitals. The most authentic records on Song building construction and detailing, the Ying Zuo Fa Shi 营做法式 (construction methods), written by Li Jie 李诫 in 1103 AD, also contain evidence that the choice of auspicious sites was considered very important during the Song period.

The selection of burial sites was also influenced by Kan Yu. The emperors of the Five Dynasties were buried in tombs on hilly sites in Luo Zhou Xian facing the south with the hills to the north, and the Emperor of the Xia dynasty, Da Yu 大禹, was buried in an auspicious site in Huiji. Qin Shi Huang Di started making preparations for his mausoleum near a summit in the hilly northern part of Li Shan soon after he became emperor.

The art of feng shui incorporates many facets of Chinese belief and culture. It refers to the Yijing (the Book of Changes), the philosophy of yin and yang (the theory of negative and positive forces), Chinese symbolism and cosmology, the theory of magnetism and some aspects of ecology, the art of landscaping and garden design, the compatibility of horoscopes and orientation and the sense of good design, both internally and externally.

The practice of feng shui involves the usage of equipment, such as the special feng shui ruler or tape and the luopan. The first luopan was probably made during the Han period by a man named Wang Chen Du who use a magnetic spoon on a diviner's board. This diviner's board was developed and it slowly evolved to the present form with a magnetic needle in the centre of a turntable of many rings of information.

Earlier luopans contained 24 directions derived from the 10 Heavenly Stems and the 12 Earthly Branches arranged in the Later Heaven Arrangement. A modern luopan is made to look attractive and mounted on a red board. Its centre, called the Heaven Pool or Tianpan, contains a south-pointing magnetic needle. The circular timber plate that is mounted around the central part is made up of three categories of information referring to the heavens, the earth and man. Twenty four directions

A building on a site with good feng shui. It has a good view and its back facing the hills. The site is enhaced by a man-made lake.

3.2 | Yijing and the eight trigrams

A feng shui luopan.

are marked in Stems, Branches and Trigrams in the three plates of Heaven, Earth and Man. The Earth plate is used to locate the qi (commonly known as the dragon) of the site. The Heaven plate is employed to locate the auspicious location with reference to the water courses and the Man plate to assess the hills.

Confucius' classic work, Yijing, the Book of Changes, was used for fortune telling and the revelation of the dangers and joys of life. The word "yi" represents the changeability of the nature of all things and the interaction and relation of the yin and yang qualities in nature. The divination of the Yijing is based on a system of ancient numerals of yin and yang which form the 64 hexagrams for reference to the Chinese system of cosmology.

The ancient numerals of the Eight Trigrams were attributed to China's first legendary emperor, Fuxi (2852 BC) who wrote the first eight trigrams, qian 乾, kun 坤, chen 辰, kan 坎, gen 艮, xun 巽, li 离, and dui 兑. Qian is represented by three solid lines indicating masculinity, the heavens, vitality and the direction northwest. Kun is shown as three broken lines representing femininity, the earth, subordination and the direction southwest. Chen appears as two broken lines and a solid line to symbolise development and change and east. Kan means danger, accident and north and it is represented by a solid line sandwiched by two broken lines. Gen symbolises halt, obstacle and northeast, and it is represented by a solid and two broken lines. Xun is equated to influence, possibility, change and southeast, and it is shown as one broken and two solid lines. Li may be interpreted as quality, firmness, and the south, denoted by a broken line sandwiched between two solid lines. Dui means happiness,

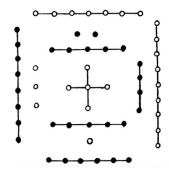

Hetu
The Hetu consists of 55 dots with numbers 1 through 10.

satisfaction and west, and is indicated by one broken and two solid lines.

The ancient numerical symbols, called the Hetu, were first observed by Fuxi on the back of a mythical animal on the Yellow River, and consisted of 55 dots which were translated into the Eight Trigrams. By multiplying the number 8 eightfold the 64 Hexagrams were formed.

Another legendary leader called Yu saw the trigrams formulated by dots on the back of a huge tortoise on the Le River during the time of the great floods. The dots were made in black and white (yin and yang). This arrangement of the Trigrams was later studied and interpreted by Wen Wang (1231–1135 BC), the first emperor of the Zhou dynasty, in a cyclical formation: qian 乾, kan 坎, gen 艮, chen 辰, xun 巽, li 离, kun 坤, dui 兑. Since then the Chinese have identified the symbols of the trigrams with the signs of the cosmos which were incorporated into the practice of kan yu or feng shui as astrological concepts and

earthly geographical features. The cardinal points of orientation and the Five Elements (Gold 金, Wood 木, Water 水, Fire 火 and Earth 土) were represented by the Trigrams. Gold is represented by West, Wood East, Water North, Fire South and Earth Central.

In the Hetu diagram the elements and orientations are associated to numbers as follows: Gold/West to 4,9; Wood/East to 3,8; Water/North to 1,6; Fire/South to 2,7; and Earth/Central to 5. Since each element and direction is represented by an odd (yang 阳) and an even (yin 阴) number it is productive (as yang and yin produces) and in harmony (for the significance of numbers, see Lip: 1992). This system of arrangement of the Hetu is called

The 64 Hexagrams were derived from the 8 Trigrams. Each of the Trigrams is made up of a yin (a broken--) and a young (an unbroken-)line. By combining one of the Trigrams with another the 64 Hexagrams are formed as shown in the diagram. These Hexagrams are used in the Yijing to symbolise the 64 possible situations of divination or fortune telling

Former Heaven Trigrams. An improvement of this system was made and the Former Heaven Trigrams were read with the Later Heaven Trigrams to achieve a balanced view of the heavenly concept and the earthly forces and so the combined system was used by many geomancers for the arrangement of physical elements and spaces. It is important to bear in mind that the relationship of elements, orientations and numbers is not to be taken literally but rather the hidden significance of cosmological influences. For example, in Chinese mythology and belief the ruler of the heavens was said to rule the portion facing south and so south has always been regarded as an auspicious direction even though each individual, according to his horoscope, has his own favourite orientation for his front door and his bed. South is given so much importance that ancient maps were drawn "upside down", with south at the top.

From the Eight Trigrams the 64 Hexagrams were derived and these Hexagrams and their significances are shown in the chart below.

Chart showing the relationship of the five elements the organ, taste, colours and sensory organs

Organs	Taste	Colours	Sensory Organs	Elements
liver	sour	green	eye	wood
heart	bitter	red	tongue	fire
spleen	sweet	yellow	mouth	earth
lung	metallic	white	nose	gold
kidney	salty	black	ear	water

The compatible elements are paired accordingly:

Water with Wood
Wood with Fire
Fire with Earth
Earth with Gold
Gold with Water

The incompatible elements are:

Earth with Water
Water with Fire
Fire with Gold
Gold with Wood
Wood with Earth

3.3 | The five elements and ganzhi

The theory and balance of yin, yang and the Five Elements is central to Chinese thinking. The concept that man benefits from the balance and harmony of yin and yang in all things is based on cosmological theory while the concept of the workings of the Five Elements is seen in the physical world and in nature. According to the Chinese sages all things in the physical world can be classified under the Five Elements of Gold, Wood, Water, Fire and Earth. These elements are closely associated with natural things and forces. Gold is associated with the west, the autumn, and the colour white; Wood with the east, the spring and the colour green; Water with the north, winter and the colour black; Fire with the south, the summer and the colour red; and Earth with the central position and the colour yellow. Thus the Five Elements are like the seasons, succeeding one another in a cycle of either production or destruction as shown in the diagram below.

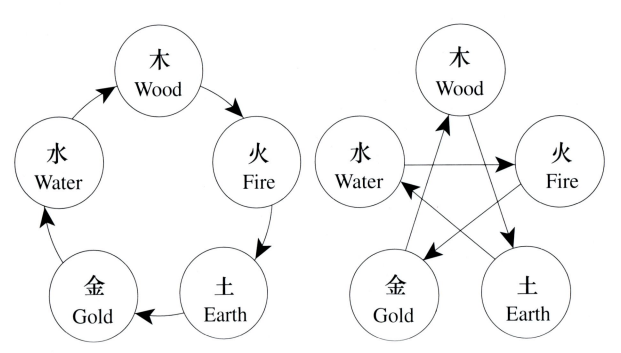

The Five Elements
The working of the Five Elements is shown in the diagrams. The diagram on the left shows the productivity and the diagram on the right shows the destructivity.

Animal Symbols
The rat, the ox, the tiger, the rabbit, the dragon, the snake, the horse, the goat, the monkey, the rooster, the dog and the pig.

The Eight Trigrams were related to the Ganzhi 干支 system in which the Ten Heavenly Stems were combined with the Twelve Earthly Branches to form the cyclical 60 sexagenary lunar recurrent years. The Ganzhi system of identifying each year with a horoscopic animal symbol was first invented by the minister of the first emperor of China in 2697 BC. A list showing the Ganzhi and horoscopes in sequential order is: bingzi 丙子 (rat), dingchou 丁丑 (ox), wuyin 戊寅 (tiger), jimao 己卯 (rabbit), gengchen 庚辰 (dragon), xinsi 辛巳 (snake), renwu 壬午 (horse), kuiwei 癸未 (goat), jiashen 甲申 (monkey), yiyou 乙酉 (rooster), bingshu 丙戌 (dog), dinghai 丁亥 (pig), wuzi 戊子 (rat), jichou 己丑 (ox), gengyin 庚寅 (tiger), xinmao 辛卯 (rabbit), renchen 壬辰 (dragon), kuisi 癸巳 (snake), jiawu 甲午 (horse), yiwei 乙未 (goat), bingshen 丙申 (monkey), dingyou 丁酉 (rooster), wushu 戊戌 (dog), jihai 己亥 (pig), gengzi 庚子 (rat), xinchou 辛丑 (ox), renyin 壬寅 (tiger), kuimao 癸卯 (rabbit), jiachen 甲辰 (dragon), yisi 乙巳 (snake), bingwu 丙午 (horse), dingwei 丁未 (goat), wushen 戊申 (monkey), jiyou 己酉 (rooster), gengshu 庚戌 (dog), xinhai 辛亥 (pig), renzi 壬子 (rat), kuichou 癸丑 (ox), jiayin 甲寅 (tiger), yimao 乙卯 (rabbit), bingchen 丙辰 (dragon), dingsi 丁巳 (snake), wuwu 戊午 (horse), jiwei 己未 (goat), gengshen 庚申 (monkey), xinyou 辛酉 (rooster), renshu 壬戌 (dog), kuihai 癸亥 (pig), jiazi 甲子 (rat), yichou 乙丑 (ox), bingyin 丙寅 (tiger), dingmao 丁卯 (rabbit), wuchen 戊辰 (dragon), jisi 己巳 (snake), gengwu 庚午 (horse), xinwei 辛未 (goat), renshen 壬申 (monkey), kuiyou 癸酉 (rooster), jiashu 甲戌 (dog) and yihai 乙亥 (pig). From this list it can be seen that the 60 year cycle called *Jiazi Nian* (wood rat year of the celestial stem and earthly branch) is made up of a unit of the Earthly Branch and a unit of the Heavenly Stem.

Mountain and qi
Mountains and sea are sources of qi. In ancient times and during the Ming and Qing dynasties Emperors
ascended the mountains to get rejuvenated by the qi.

3.4 | The philosophy of the yin and yang

To the Chinese, yin represents the female, the moon, night, darkness, negativity, softness, valleys and all feminine qualities. Yang denotes the male, the sun, day, brightness, positiveness, hardness, hills and all masculine qualities. All things under the sky can be classified as yin or yang. When there is perfect balance of the yin and yang ingredients and qualities in things, growth flourishes and "sheng qi" 生气 (good cosmic breath or energy of the earth) enhances the environment.

It is believed that there is "qi" (breath of the earth) or energy in the earth, in all living things and in the environment. If the qi is rejuvenating it is called "sheng qi" 生气 but if it is stifling it is called "si qi" 死气 (breath of death or decay). Thus when a living thing dies it is filled with si qi. But if a living thing is filled with sheng qi it is full of energy and vitality. An expert in Chinese martial arts is by definition well versed in qigong (the training of qi in the body) and should be extremely agile and energetic, full of life and vitality. This balance also helps to explain the cure performed by an acupuncturist, when inserting a needle into the meridian points of the body of an ill person to activate the qi in the body. Besides reinforcing the physical strength of a person qi stimulates the mind and balances the emotional well-being. A geomancer locates the "sheng qi" or good cosmic energy of the earth and utilises it to benefit man. This cosmic energy infuses all living things and revitalizes man's energy to achieve the balance of yin and yang of things on earth.

The belief of the balance of the yin and yang in nature was reinforced during the 3rd century BC especially during the Zhou period when the yin/yang schools flourished. The growth of all living things on the earth and the productivity in nature were attributed to the theory of the harmonious union of yin and yang elements and qualities. Yin is closely related to and complimentary to yang. It was believed to be important to achieve the balance of yin and yang in the workings of the Five Elements, the numbers, the placement of the natural and man-made elements, the siting of buildings, and in all things. When something was too yin it became yang and when it was too yang it turned yin. The integration of the yin and yang of the Trigrams resulted in the creation of the 64 Hexagrams as shown in the diagram below. It was essential to maintain

a perfect balance or inequilibrium would result in undesirable changes in both the physical and natural environments.

Chart showing the yin and yang of the things in nature and in physical form or activity.

Nature/ Physical Form	Yin	Yang
Seasons	Autumn, Winter	Spring, Summer
Time	night	day
Astronomy	moon	sun
Time	night	day
Gender	female	male
Nature	water/moisture/ coolness	hill/solid state/ heat
Elements	Metal/Water	Wood/Fire
Physical body	lower part of body	upper part of body
Organs	liver, heart, spleen, lung, kidney	stomach, bladder

3.5 | Symbolism and cosmology

Many writers and scholars have researched into the Chinese concept of cosmology and celestial patterns. They have derived four emblems in the celestial heavens as the Azure Dragon, the White Tiger, the Black Turtle and the Red Bird. These emblems are associated with the directions as follows: Black Turtle = North; Azure Dragon = East; Red Bird = South and White Tiger = West. In feng

Animal symbolism.

shui it is important to ensure that the left, the Azure Dragon, is higher than the right, the White Tiger, and that the back, the Black Turtle, is higher than the front, the Red Bird.

The 12 stellar positions corresponded to the 12 regions of the Chinese tributary sites on earth and these positions were related to the 12 Earthly Branches which were used as a cycle of 12 symbolical animals in Chinese horoscopes. The other cycle of the Ten Heavenly Stems combining with that of the Twelve Branches made up the cycle of 60 years called Jiazi Nian. The orientation of the main door of a building is to be decided according to the date of completion of the building with reference to the Jiazi Nian, the particular year in the 60-year sexagenary cycle.

The Nine Essences or influences first mentioned by Fu Xi were classified in terms of Orientation, Colour and Element as follows:

	Colour	Orientation	Element
1	White	North	Water
2	Black	Southwest	Earth
3	Greenish blue	East	Wood
4	Green	Southeast	Wood
5	Yellow	Central	Earth
6	White	Northwest	Gold
7	Red	West	Gold
8	White	Northeast	Earth
9	Purple	South	Fire

It can be seen that the orientation of a building is not determined solely on the birthdate of the owner. Other considerations such as the relationship of the building to the essence, element, surrounding buildings and natural landscape features as well as with the Nine Stars are just as important. The Nine Stars, namely Tan Lang 貪狼 (meaning literally 'covetous heavenly wolf'), Ju Men 巨门 (large door), Lu Cun 禄存 (preserved wealth), Wen Qu 文曲 (song of the educated), Lian Zhen 廉真 (honest and pure), Wu Qu 武曲 (song of the military), Po Jun 破军 (broken army), Zuo Fu 左辅 (left reinforcement) and You Bi 右弼 (right assistant). The first two stars are under Jupiter, the third and eighth Saturn, the fourth and ninth Mercury, the fifth Mars and the sixth and seventh Venus. These stars are also classified under the Elements as shown below:

Stars	Elements	Auspicious/Inauspicious	
Tan Lang	Wood	x	
Ju Men	Earth	x	
Lu Cun	Earth		x
Wen Qu	Water		x
Lian Zhen	Fire		x
Wu Qu	Gold	x	
Po Jun	Gold		x
Zuo Fu	Earth		
You Bi	Water	unfixed	

The location and orientation of a building is made with reference to the Nine Stars. The site on which the building sits is subdivided into 24 parts as qian 乾, kun 坤, gen 艮, xun 巽, yin 寅, shen 申, shu 戌, hai 亥, chen 辰, ji 己, chou 丑, wei 未, yi 乙, xin 辛, kui 癸, ding 丁, jia 甲, geng 庚, bing 丙, ren 壬, zi 子, wu 午, mao 卯, and you 酉.

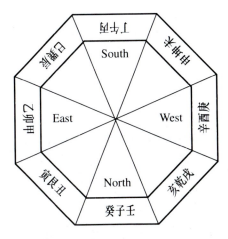

24 directions for orientation.

For thousands of years the Chinese have been prejudiced against the northeast and southwest as these directions are lacking in spirits of both heavenly and earthly essence.

Doing the right thing at the right time and at the right place is also an important consideration in feng shui because the cyclical movements and changes influence the harmonious disposition of things on earth and affect the entry of auspicious qi to the buildings. This belief is clearly stated in the Kao Gong Ji Tu 考工记图 published in 1955 in Changsha, China. The Tong Shu, the Chinese Almanac, contains a lunar calendar which gives data for the choice of day and time for activities that bring in good consequences and auspicious qi.

Symbols used on roof eaves include inverted lotus buds, phoenixes, pearls, flowers etc.

It is believed that the Chinese were the first to have discovered the magnetism in the earth. In the 11th century Shen Kuo (1031–1095 AD), a Chinese mathematician and instrument maker, first made records of the use of a magnetic compass, and the first seafarer's compass was then invented. This was later improved upon with many layers of information related to cosmology and feng shui. It was noted that the magnetic poles exerted forces on each other, north and south poles attracting and like poles repelling each other. Magnetism could result in atomic interaction. In feng shui terms the blood circulation and health of a person may be affected by adverse magnetic influences.

It has long been established that there is a close relationship between living things and their environment, and that there is a need to conserve natural resources and the environment. As living species are inseparable from the built and natural environments man must strive to survive best in a particular habitat for food, shelter and success. The Chinese explain the

Colour symbolism - Red for happiness, yellow royalty, black solemnness, green longevity and blue heavenly blessings.

natural forces such as climate and weather, the influence of vegetation, geographical features such as hills and valleys and water courses on their habitats in terms of feng shui. For example, soil erosion is a poor kan yu feature and so building on land subject to significant soil erosion will eventually lead to disaster.

Hills are sources of qi and raw materials. At the eastern part of the Great Wall of China at the Shan Hai Guan in the province of Hebei are ranges of the Yan Shan which are noted for their auspicious feng shui qualities with the hills to the north and the sea to the south. In the northwestern region of Hunan there is an excellent area called Zhang Jia Ji. There are ranges of hills 3000 feet high and fertile valleys with hundreds of reflective rivers which bring sheng qi (breath of life) to the area. The most well known of the hills is the Huang Si Zai which resembles a strong male lion sitting on a range of hills guarding the entire area. In the central part of Hunan is a famous feng shui hill named Heng Shan which is most imposing and noted for its breathtaking waterfalls and rejuvenating qi. The Qing Liang Shan in Nanjing and the Yi He Yuan in Beijing are complexes on hills designed with many auspicious kan yu features.

Rivers may also be sources of qi provided they are meandering and flow slowly. The huanghe (Yellow River) however, has always been a poor feng shui influence as it has caused countless calamities to those who dwell along its banks.

SYMBOLISM

The symbolism of decorative elements has to be understood in its usage. Some elements and their symbolism are listed below:

Elements of decoration	Symbolism
bamboo	youthfulness/longevity
bat	good luck/joy
gourd-shaped bottle	capture of evil influence
carp	success/wishes come true
peach	beauty/joy
chrysanthemum	endurance/longevity
cloud pattern	blessings/happiness
crane	longevity/wisdom
cypress	longevity/strength
deer	wealth
dragon	royalty/power
elephant	wisdom
fan	goodness
flute	disappear
goose	marital bliss
hill	backing
jade	purity
lion	power/repellence of evil
lotus	uprightness/endurance
peony	success
phoenix	yin quality/beauty
pine	longevity
plum	endurance/purity
pomegranate	fertility
square	earth/stability
taiji symbol	perfect balance of yin and yang
tortoise	longevity
triangle	instability
unicorn	wisdom
water	wealth/source of breath
willow	Spring/gentleness

The above is a short list of decorative elements and symbols which can be used in decorative art and building symbols. Their usage must be correctly applied or else the feng shui of symbols will be misunderstood.

The hula on top of the roof repels evil spirits. Bamboo tiles depict evergreen and longevity.

3.6 | Horoscopes

The Chinese believe that the moment a child is born his fate can be read with reference to the year, month, day and time of his birth, the Elements of Birth (see Lip: 1988, for charts which enable one to find the Elements of Birth). From the Elements of Birth one is able to determine which elements one is compatible with where the orientation of one's bed is concerned. It is a common practice to assess the element of birth of the house owner and the element of birth of the house (the date of completion of the house) and ensure that the Elements do not clash. For ease of reference charts are shown below to demonstrate the difference in orientation for males and females.

FAVOURABLE ORIENTATIONS

Orientation: North
Males born in: 1927, 1936, 1945, 1954, 1963, 1972, 1981, 1990.............................
Females born in: 1923, 1932, 1941, 1950, 1959, 1968, 1977, 1986, 1995 ....

Orientation: Northeast
Males born in: 1929, 1938, 1947, 1956, 1965, 1974, 1983, 1992.........................
Females born in: 1930, 1939, 1948, 1957, 1966, 1975, 1984, 1993............................

Orientation: East
Males and females born in: 1925, 1934, 1943, 1952, 1961, 1970, 1979, 1988, 1997...........

Orientation Southeast
Males born in: 1924, 1933, 1942, 1951, 1960, 1969, 1978, 1987, 1996..............................
Females born in: 1926, 1935, 1944, 1953, 1962, 1971, 1980, 1989, 1998 ....

Orientation: South
Males born in: 1928, 1937, 1946, 1955, 1964, 1973, 1982, 1991 ....
Females born in: 1922, 1931, 1940, 1949, 1958, 1967, 1976, 1985, 1994 ....

Orientation Southwest
Males born in: 1923, 1932, 1941, 1950, 1959, 1968, 1977, 1986, 1995..........................
Females born in: 1924, 1933, 1942, 1951, 1960, 1969, 1978, 1987, 1996 ....

Orientation: West
Males born in: 1921, 1930, 1939, 1948, 1957, 1966, 1975, 1984, 1993...............................
Females born in: 1920, 1929, 1938, 1947, 1956, 1965, 1974, 1983, 1992 ....

Orientation: Northwest
Males born in: 1922, 1931, 1940, 1949, 1958, 1967, 1976, 1985, 1994.............................
Females born in: 1928, 1937, 1946, 1955, 1964, 1973, 1982, 1991.............................

(Note that the age difference of males or females in a row is 9 years. Therefore it is easy to refer to the charts to find out the orientation of those born after 1998.)

Chart showing the animal symbols, years of birth, elements and binomials:

The Animal	The Year	The Element	(Binomials)
1. The Rat	10/2/1948 – 28/1/1949	fire	(Wu Zi)
	28/1/1960 – 14/2/1961	earth	(Geng Zi)
	15/2/1972 – 02/2/1973	wood	(Ren Zi)
	02/2/1984 – 19/2/1985	gold	(Jia Zi)
	19/2/1996 – 06/2/1997	water	(Bing Zi)
2. The Ox	29/1/1949 – 16/2/1950	fire	(Ji Chou)
	15/2/1961 – 04/2/1962	earth	(Xin Chou)
	03/2/1973 – 22/1/1974	wood	(Kui Chou)
	20/2/1985 – 08/2/1986	gold	(Yi Chou)
	07/2/1997 – 27/1/1998	water	(Ding Chou)
3. The Tiger	17/2/1950 – 05/2/1951	wood	(Geng Yin)
	05/2/1962 – 24/1/1963	gold	(Ren Yin)
	23/1/1974 – 10/2/1975	water	(Jia Yin)
	09/2/1986 – 28/1/1987	fire	(Bing Yin)
	28/1/1998 – 15/2/1999	earth	(Wu Yin)
4. The Rabbit	06/2/1951 – 26/1/1952	wood	(Xin Mao)
	25/1/1963 – 12/2/1964	gold	(Kui Mao)
	11/2/1975 – 30/1/1976	water	(Yi Mao)
	29/1/1987 – 16/2/1988	fire	(Ding Mao)
	16/2/1999 – 04/2/2000	earth	(Ji Mao)
5. The Dragon	08/2/1940 – 26/1/1941	gold	(Geng Chen)
	27/2/1952 – 13/2/1953	water	(Ren Chen)
	13/2/1964 – 01/2/1965	fire	(Jia Chen)
	31/1/1976 – 17/2/1977	earth	(Bing Chen)
	17/2/1988 – 05/2/1989	wood	(Wu Chen)
	05/2/2000 – 23/1/2001		
6. The Snake	27/1/1941 – 14/2/1942	gold	(Xin Si)
	14/2/1953 – 02/2/1954	water	(Kui Si)
	02/2/1965 – 20/1/1966	fire	(Yi Si)
	18/2/1977 – 06/2/1978	earth	(Ding Si)
	06/2/1989 – 26/1/1990	wood	(Ji Si)
	24/1/2001 – 11/2/2002		

The Animal	The Year	The Element	(Binomials)
7. The Horse	15/2/1942 – 4/2/1943	wood	(Ren Wu)
	03/2/1954 – 23/1/1955	gold	(Jia Wu)
	04/1/1966 – 08/2/1967	water	(Bing Wu)
	07/2/1978 – 27/1/1979	fire	(Wu Wu)
	27/1/1990 – 14/2/1991	earth	(Geng Wu)
8. The Goat	05/2/1943 – 24/1/1944	wood	(Kui Wei)
	24/1/1955 – 11/2/1956	gold	(Yi Wei)
	09/2/1967 – 29/1/1968	water	(Ding Wei)
	28/1/1979 – 15/1/1980	fire	(Ji Wei)
	15/2/1991 – 03/2/1992	earth	(Xin Wei)
9. The Monkey	25/1/1944 – 12/2/1945	water	(Jia Shen)
	12/2/1956 – 30/1/1957	fire	(Bing Shen)
	30/1/1968 – 16/2/1969	earth	(Wu Shen)
	16/2/1980 – 04/2/1981	wood	(Geng Shen)
	04/2/1992 – 22/1/1993	gold	(Ren Shen)
10. The Rooster	13/2/1945 – 01/2/1946	water	(Yi You)
	31/1/1957 – 17/2/1958	fire	(Ding You)
	17/2/1969 – 05/2/1970	earth	(Ji You)
	05/2/1981 – 24/1/1982	wood	(Xin You)
	23/1/1993 – 09/2/1994	gold	(Kui You)
11. The Dog	02/2/1946 – 21/1/1947	earth	(Bing Shu)
	18/2/1958 – 07/2/1959	wood	(Wu Shu)
	06/2/1970 – 26/1/1971	gold	(Geng Shu)
	25/1/1982 – 12/2/1983	water	(Ren Shu)
	10/2/1994 – 30/1/1995	fire	(Jia Shu)
12. The Pig	22/1/1947 – 09/2/1948	earth	(Ding Hai)
	08/2/1959 – 27/1/1960	wood	(Ji Hai)
	27/1/1971 – 14/2/1972	gold	(Xin Hai)
	13/2/1983 – 01/2/1984	water	(Kui Hai)
	31/1/1995 – 18/2/1996	fire	(Yi Hai)

Note: A binomial consists of 2 Chinese characters taken from the Heavenly Stems and the Earthly Branches. See Lip, Evelyn, *Fun with Chinese Horoscopes*, Graham Brash Pte Ltd, Singapore 1981, for compatibility of animal symbols.

江村即事
jiāng cūn jí shì

司空曙
sī kōng shǔ

罢	钓	归	来	不	系	船,
bà	diào	guī	lái	bù	jì	chuán
江	村	月	落	正	堪	眠。
jiāng	cūn	yuè	luò	zhèng	kān	mián
纵	然	一	夜	风	吹	去,
zòng	rán	yī	yè	fēng	chuī	qù
只	在	芦	花	浅	水	边。
zhǐ	zài	lú	huā	qián	shuǐ	biān

This Tang poem written by Si Kong Shu describes the scenic beauty of a village.
"the reeds grow...
the water shallow..."

CONTENTS

73

4.1 | Temples and traditions

Traditional Chinese teaching informs social behaviour, and Chinese temples have always been used for the teaching and expression of these values. The Chinese congregate in temples and religious centres during festive seasons to worship their gods and ancestors, and to meet socially as clans or as devotees who share the same religious aspirations.

In terms of religious architecture throughout the world the roof forms, wall and roof decorations, colour schemes and finishing materials of Chinese temples are highly distinctive. Egyptian and Greek temples were built mainly of stone, while the material used for the basic structures of Chinese temples has always been timber. The spatial organisation, character and decoration of Chinese temples are also different from Cambodian, Burmese or Hindu temples which are essentially elaborations on the stupa idea and are designed to be admired chiefly from the outside. The Chinese temple builder's approach to the creation of space is not simply functional; it is also intended to induce an emotional reaction through the association of different kinds of spaces — semi-enclosed, enclosed and open. The aesthetic impact of the prayer hall is felt through the arrangement of the various elements such as the curved surfaces of the ceiling, with its carved beams and wooden sculptures, and the eaves and verge overhangs.

Temple architecture in China is deeply rooted in her rich culture and long history. The first major Buddhist temple, Bai Ma Si 白马寺 (White Horse Temple), was dated 67 AD and was based on the Chinese palace and official residence. The architecture of Chinese temples has not changed substantially since the 7th century AD. The planning was, and still is, based on the precepts of feng shui, in terms of symmetry and the courtyard concept, even though the structural and supporting systems have been gradually evolving since the Tang dynasty.

Roof symbols.

The architecture of China developed over, and was somehow constrained by, thousands of years of Chinese feudal tradition. As a result, constructional systems, material application and detailing techniques did not change very much. Although feudal rulers changed from one period to the next, the basic concepts behind planning and construction continued. The courtyard plan and the beam-frame structure prevailed in China and other places such as Taiwan, Korea, Vietnam, Malaysia and Singapore.

4.2 | Temple architecture

By the Han dynasty (206 BC) Chinese architecture was already well established. Thousands of temples have been built since then. One of the largest and most elaborate of

A Chinese temple on high ground.

Taihe Dian, a magnificent palace, built for the Qing emperors and modeled on traditional Chinese architecture as well as based on the principles of feng shui practice

monasteries, built during the Northern Wei period, was the Yun Ling Si 云灵寺. Since then, the technique of temple building was passed on from one generation to another. During the Qing dynasty, the Ministry of Works produced a publication on the subject of Chinese construction methods based on Li Jie's 李诚 thesis written in 1097 AD. These publications became the standard manuals for builders.

The designs of palaces, official buildings, temples and residences were in general similar in planning and were based on the courtyard plan with strict adherence to the precepts of feng shui, symmetry, axiality and wall enclosure. Such can be found in the temples and palatial buildings in the Forbidden City (see photographic illustrations in the following pages). Large temples were designed with successive internal courts enclosed by blocks of buildings. The entry to the first court was called shan men 山门 (gate of hill). On the right and left of the court were the bell and drum towers. Across the court was the tian wang dian 天王殿 (hall of the heavenly kings) beyond which was the da xiong bao dian 大雄宝殿 (main hall). Beyond the main hall was the hou dian (rear hall).

The building of temples facing the sea has been a traditional geomantic practice of the Chinese since 3,000 years ago, and this auspicious orientation is still considered important.

The roof of a Chinese temple was supported by built-up trusses, consisting of beams of diminishing length placed one over the other between timber columns, and separated from each other by short struts. Above the beams and purlins, rafters supported the tiling boards and battens and the roof tiles. The columns and framework were tied together by longitudinal beams and transverse beams. Eaves posts were built around the temple underneath the eaves to support a substantial overhang and the dou gong 斗拱 (brackets).

Since the Han dynasty the rank of a temple was reflected by its roof form and there were 4 types of roof: the gabled, the hipped, the half-hipped/half gabled and the pyramidal. Sometimes the ridge design was composed of dancing dragons flanking the blazing pearl. The fascia of a bamboo glazed tiled roof was an intricate design based on traditional patterns.

All the gable and partition walls were non-structural. The nave bay was distinct not only in plan but also in elevation and roof treatment. In Southeast Asian countries Chinese temples were based on those found in South China because of the close relationship between the Chinese abbots in South China and those in Southeast Asia and other parts where there were Chinese immigrants during the 19th century AD. During the 19th century immigrants from South China brought their religions, cultural and traditional practices as well as their building technology to Southeast Asia. The roofs of the existing temples in these areas bear evidence that they have their origin in South China because their ridge curvatures are pronounced and tilt upwards towards the gable ends just like their counterparts in South China. Temple roof ridges in Northern China are rigid and less decorative than those in the South.

Zhonghe Dian and Baohe Dian in the Forbidden City, Beijing. Zhonghe Dian was built in 1420 as a palace for the emperor to rest between periods of administration. Baohe Dian was the main royal and offical banquet hall.

The circular roof of this magnificent temple, Qi Niandian, is covered with glazed blue tiles to symbolise the heavens

4.3 | Development of Chinese temple architecture outside China

Most temples constructed in Southeast Asian regions during the 19th century were built by craftsmen from the south of China with imported materials. Temples built in the 20th century may be divided into 4 types. The first type consists of those based on the authentic Chinese style, is planned with reference to the traditional symmetry and beam frame structures, having curved roof ridges and tilted corner ribs. The second type consists of temples based on the Chinese style with some Western influences. These temples have certain Chinese features such as a symmetrical layout and a traditional roof form, but the structural and decorative elements are of reinforced concrete rather than timber. The third type consists of those temples made of timber but which are not based on the authentic Chinese style. Local methods have been used in their construction. The fourth type consists mainly of temples which were originally domestic buildings and have been converted.

The Chinese settlement in Taiwan began in the 14th century during the Ming dynasty. But the Chinese influence in Thailand, Malaysia and Singapore were not evident until the later part of the 18th century, even though in Chinese annals there are records of Zheng He

郑和, the Ming court official and explorer, making a tour to the Southseas in 1408 AD.

The first Chinese Buddhist temple in Indonesia, Jinde Yuan 金德院, was built in Batavia in 1650 AD. Malaysia's first Chinese temple, Qinghong Ting 清红亭 in Malacca, was built in the early 19th century.

As mentioned earlier, Chinese temples in the region were influenced by southern Chinese architecture because of the close ties with the abbots in South China. But in 1942 when the Asia Pacific War broke out and the People's Republic of China was formed, migration out of China was stopped. The supply of building materials and workers out of China dwindled and so southern Chinese influence declined.

At the turn of the 20th century the planning and construction of Chinese temples varied. By 1930 reinforced concrete had been introduced and incorporated in the construction of many temples. From then onward, owing to the rise in the cost of building materials and the unavailability of skilled craftsmen, Chinese temple architecture outside China changed substantially. These temples could not be modelled closely on those in South China as they were built by local craftsmen with local building materials, and are poor imitations, making use of reinforced concrete dou-gong or brackets and other Western features. These features appear unauthentic and even the superimposition of South Chinese features to assert the "Chineseness" such as the exaggerated ridge curvatures and highly complicated roof and ridge ornaments do not redeem them.

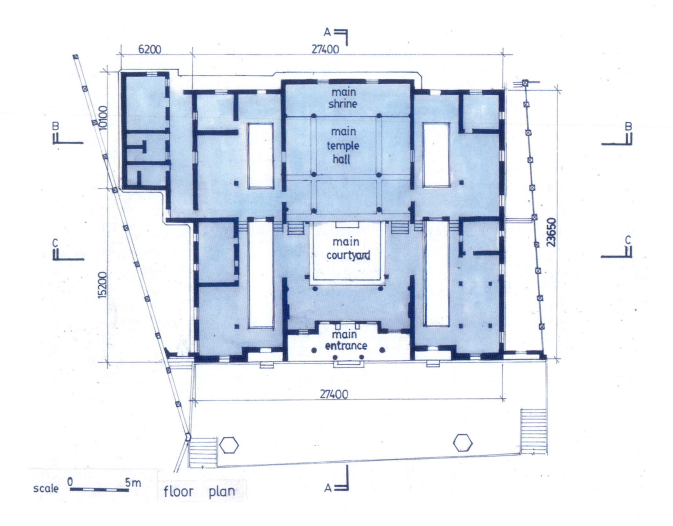

Plan of a Chinese temple outside China.

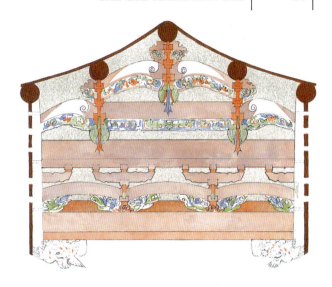

Details of a roof truss.

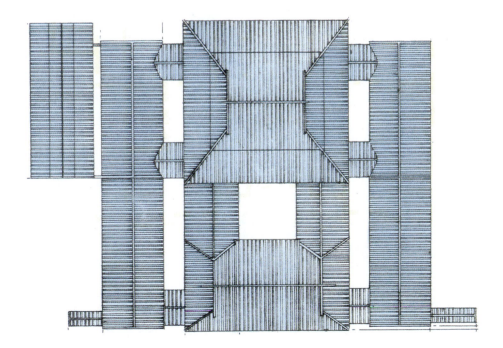

Roof plan of a Chinese temple outside China.

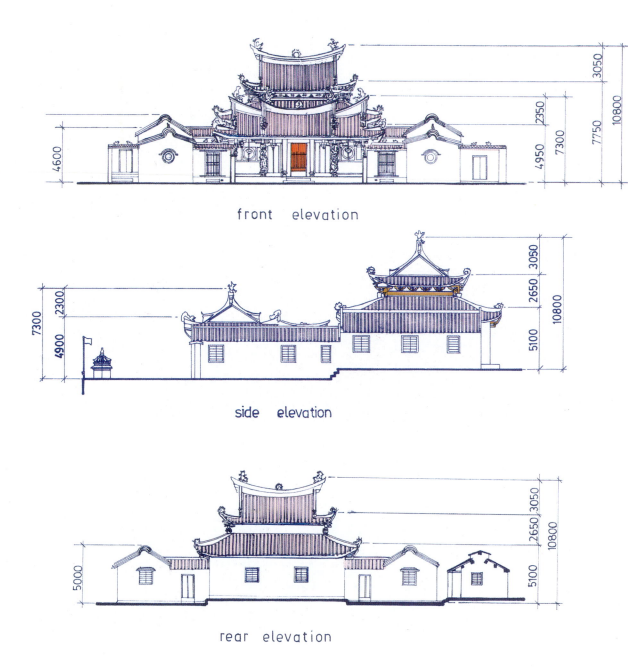

front elevation

side elevation

rear elevation

Drawings of a Chinese temple.

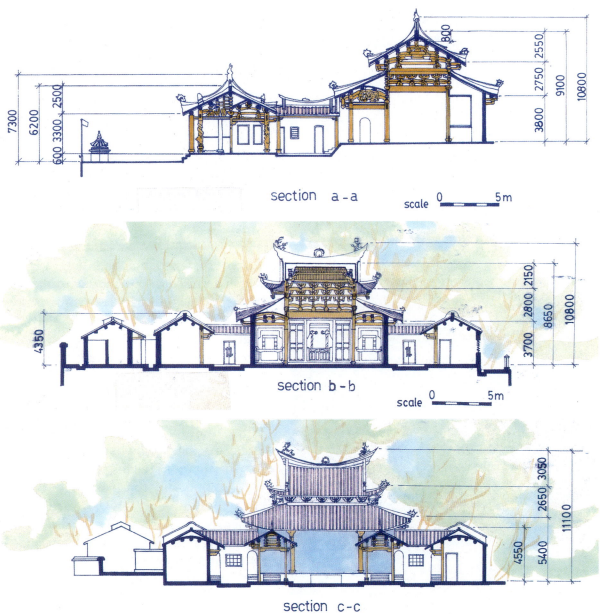

section a-a

scale 0 ___ 5m

section **b-b**

scale 0 ___ 5m

section c-c

4.4 Traditional architecture and feng shui

Many ancient Chinese cities were sited and planned with reference to the precepts of feng shui.* Beijing, which has three concentric layers of walls, was a vivid example. The palaces of the Qing era faced south. The emperor of the Qing dynasty resided in the northern part of the palatial complex and the back of his palace was against the north with the backing of the coal hill, while the

Chinese characters as symbols.

front faced south. The Altar of Heaven was enclosed by a square wall (representing earthly happiness) and a circular wall (symbolising heavenly blessings). It was built on three concentric rings of terraces paved with marble. The building elements and finishes of the altar were significant in terms of symbolism and feng shui. For example, the concentric rings of marble on the top-most terrace were arranged from 9 to 81, both being lucky numbers. The innate connection of the yin and yang elements could be seen in this traditional architectural structure.

Traditional Chinese architecture is closely related to feng shui and yin/yang concepts which are used to present dualism and balance. In fact it is said that feng shui is so deeply rooted in Chinese architecture that since historic times it has been incorporated into architectural planning and decorative motifs. It has been used for the choice and shaping of building sites. Its theory, being based on Chinese natural philosophy, provides rational explanation for the planning concepts of symmetry, balance, discipline, wall-enclosure, correct orientation (facing the sea with higher background) and courtyard layout so that the built environment may be ordered and controlled. Several examples of traditional Chinese buildings complete with sections and decorative motifs are shown in the previous pages.

Chinese buildings are sited so as to be in harmony with nature and to receive qi from auspicious directions. Qi is most vibrant in

*This point is elaborated on in *Feng Shui and Business* (Lip, Evelyn, Times Books International, Singapore)

areas which face the sea with mountains to the rear, because in such a situation the heavenly and earthly qi are able to interact with each other. The high land at the rear acts as a protective shield against undesirable natural forces. The lower front facing the sea benefits from the scenic views and taps qi from the sea. Ideally an auspicious site for a traditional building is one which corresponds to the four quadrants so that the North and the Black Turtle is highest; the left and East, being the Azure Dragon, is higher than the right or West, (the White Tiger); and the South, the Red Bird, is lowest and ideally facing a pond or lake or slow moving river or calm sea. In most of China's old cities and villages the familiar phenomena of feng shui features are apparent.

The siting of a building or a group of buildings requires that a geomancer study the topography of the entire site and the physical features of the surrounding sites. The "qi" (breath of the earth) and the "long" (the pulse of the site) have to be assessed. Therefore the soil condition, the flow of water courses and the formation of the land must be noted. The location of the "long" is sometimes known as the detection of the "shan" 山, "ju" 局, "ge" 格, "wei" 位 and "xiang" 向. Shan is assessed from the study of the relationship of the natural topography to the siting of the building. Ju is obtained by studying the relationship of the water courses and the location of the building. Ge is assessed by studying the relationship of the surrounding physical elements with the building. Wei is determined by the relationship of the neighbouring buildings to the proposed building. Xiang refers to the orientation of the building itself. Good "ju" and "sheng qi" (revitalizing breath) are essential and they enhance good feng shui.

A building does not exist by itself as it has to relate to the rest of the urban fabric, physical elements, roads and other environmental factors.

Xiang 向
The orientation of a building is of vital importance as it affects the built and internal environment.

4.5 | Landscape and garden design

The art of landscaping and garden design was expressed in imperial as well as in private or public gardens. One of the most elaborate imperial gardens ever built was the Li Gong, the informal residence of the Han dynasty emperor. By the Jin dynasty (3rd century) private gardens also became elaborate and large in scale. During the Tang period garden design reached its climax both in scale and in style. Garden design flourished even more during the Song dynasty when the 10 most impressive gardens were built in Xihu 西湖. By the Qing dynasty many areas such as Jiangnan, Suzhou and Hangzhou were well known for their beautiful landscaped gardens with good feng shui.

The essence of the famous gardens is demonstrated by the presence of "qi", the breath of life. Qi is achieved by siting the garden on auspicious sites with natural landscape elements such as hills, rivers and lakes. The entire garden is designed in such a way that every element, be it natural or man-made, blends with nature and the geographical character of the site so that every hill, valley, built structure, corridor, pavilion and plant is in harmony with other elements and the site. The skill of balancing yin and yang elements to achieve an equilibrium is apparent in Chinese garden design. The "yang hill" contrasts vividly with the "yin valley" while the built form ventilates through the open courtyards. The landscape elements are arranged and built in such a way that there is kai 开 (open) and he 合 (closed); dong 动 (moving) and jing 静 (stationary); shang 上 (up) and xia 下 (down); gao 高 (high) and di 低 (low). The hills make the backdrop while the water or lakes bring the "qi" and source of life.

In kan yu or feng shui theory the concept of li 理 and qi 气 on landscape explains the dual aspects of the nature of the earth. Li is the physical or form of the land while qi is the spiritual or the usage of land. In things found in the landscape there is a particular order within which harmony should exist. The arrangement of each stone, pavilion, house, corridor, plant, tree, water source and rockery must be done in accordance with li so that the qi in the "dragon vein" will not be blocked. Similarly, the water course, also called the water dragon, is introduced to reinforce and concentrate the source of qi which brings life to all living things.

The individual features of a landscape are classified into Elements according to their shapes. Squarish or rectangular shapes belong to the Earth Element while star-shaped elements are Fire. Long, flowing or curved formations are of the Water Element while long but rectangular shapes are Wood and round is Gold. Favourable and agreeable Elements are: Water (curved) with Wood (rectangular); Wood with Fire (star-shaped); Fire with Earth (squarish shaped); Earth with Gold (round) and Gold with Water. Therefore the placement of landscape elements and structures should be according to the mutually productive or favourable order. The unfavourable combinations are: Earth with Water; Water with Fire; Fire with Gold; Gold with Wood and Wood with Earth.

4.6 | Furniture

Like architecture, Chinese furniture design follows tradition. It is based on a frame system and the basic material used is timber. The structural parts are joined together with mortise and tenon joints instead of with nails and glue. In terms of decorative motifs Chinese furniture design is similar to Chinese architecture. Styles typical to the northern part of China are different from those popular in the south because of the differences in climate, social and living habits.

Although little was written on furniture making during the Shang and Qin period it is evident that furniture design was simplified but was made with some reference to Liji 礼制 and Xuanxue 玄学. It was later influenced by Confucian ideas of symmetry and balance. Nevertheless it was designed to suit the anthropometric requirements of the users who were in the habit of sitting on floor mats.

Since the Han dynasty the construction method of Chinese furniture has not changed drastically, although the details and carving has varied from one artisan to another and from one dynasty to another. By the time of the Song dynasty the Chinese no longer preferred to sit on the floor. The design of chairs and other furniture items flourished during Tang

dynasty. During the Ming period furniture design underwent a period of refinement. For example, the horse hoof (mati 马蹄) was changed to a carved leg. By the end of the Qing period furniture design had declined and become less elegant.

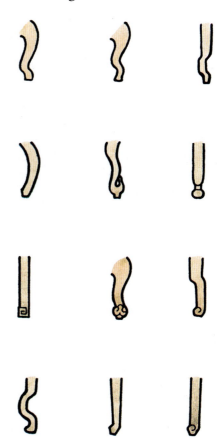

Legs of tables and chairs-
Legs of tables and chairs designed in various forms such as xia gong jiao 虾公脚, *wan jiao* 湾脚, *yang ti jiao* 羊蹄脚, *qin jiao* 琴脚, *ling zhi jiao* 灵芝脚, *ma ti jiao* 马蹄脚, *xiang mian jiao* 香绵脚, *gua dan jiao* 瓜旦脚, *mei hua jiao* 梅花脚, *si tou jiao* 狮头脚, *kan jiao* 槛脚, *zhi jiao* 直脚 *and shao cao jiano* 勺曹脚.

This photograph shows Chinese antique furniture complimented with forceful Chinese calligraphic writings.

Kou huan jie sheng 扣环结绳 *(ropes and pendant in knots).*

Kou jie sheng 扣结绳 *(ropes in knots).*

Pu ti hua heng 菩提花横 *(floral).*

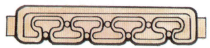

Ru yi ji xiang 如意吉祥 *(luck and success).*

Diao zhong kou sheng 吊钟扣绳 *(bells and ropes).*

The detailing of Chinese furniture is still intricate, appealing and elegant. Styles of furniture can be classified into various types such as suzhuang 苏庄, yangzhuang 洋庄, tangzhuang 唐庄, guanzhuang 官庄 and mingshi 明式. For the suzhuang style, lingzhi cao 灵芝草, jiesheng kou 结绳扣, tizhu 提竹 and meique 梅雀 are used as decorative motifs. For the yangzhuang patterns like bulian 布廉, mozhu 摸珠 and marble panels are used as decorative elements. For the tangzhuang, shitou 狮头, guadan 瓜旦 and anpai 案牌 are used. For the guanzhuang, bogu yunlu 博古匀橹 is used while for the mingshi, Ming dynasty decorative motifs are applied.

The types of timber for furniture making include heimu 黑木 or suanzhimu 酸枝木 (black wood), huali 花梨 (pear wood), hongmu 红木 (red wood), wumu 乌木 (ebony), songmu 松木 (pine), youmu 柚木 (oil wood), zhang naomu 樟瑙木 (camphor wood), sumu 苏木 (a wood named su), huangmu 黄木 (yellow wood), nanmu 楠木 (a hard wood), boluomu 波罗木 and kuandian. The most durable and popular was and still is the suanzhimu originally from Cambodia and Burma. It is classified into 4 categories, namely zitan 紫檀, heitan 黑檀, hongtan 红檀 and baitan 白檀.

Chinese furniture falls into five different types: chuang 床 (bed), gui 柜 (cupboard), yi

A Chinese bed.

Types of cupboard.

Furniture pieces.

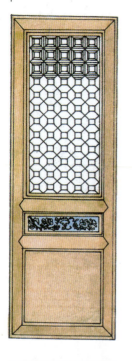

Plans, section and elevation of an armchair.

Chinese doors-
The designs carved on Chinese screens and doors are based on lucky symbols such as old coins and auspicious words like kou 口 *signifying posterity.*

椅and deng 凳 (chair) and zhao 桌 (table). These types can be subdivided according to their specific uses as follows: armchairs and tables for the living space; table and stools for the dining room; table and chairs with backs for the study; wardrobes, beds and chests for the bedrooms; cabinets, altar tables, side tables, psaltery tables and cases. Chinese furniture should be arranged in a balanced layout. In the living room the armchairs are usually in two rows along the walls of the hall. A round table and four stools can be placed in between the armchairs. Two reclining chairs can be placed near a window at the main entrance. An altar may be situated against the end wall. Couches may be placed beyond the living room.

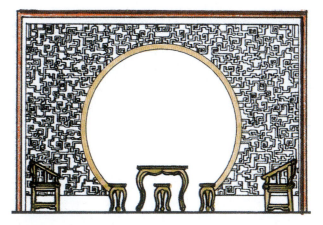

Section of the sitting hall showing the elevation of Chinese furniture.

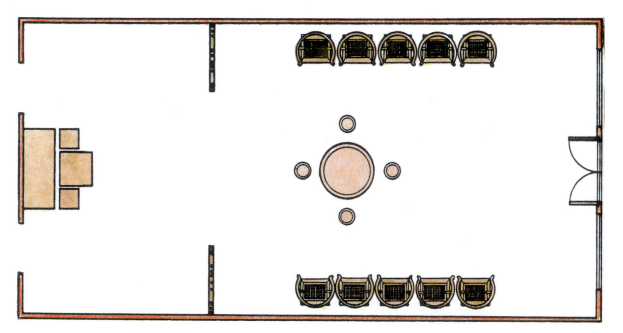

Layout of Chinese furniture in a sitting hall and in an ancestor worship hall.

Bedroom of Guang Xu
This shows the bedroom of Guang Xu 光绪, the second last emperor of the Qing dynasty.

Sitting area of Guang Xu for granting an audience.

Bedroom of Ci Xi, empress dowager of the last Qing era.

Some chuang are like large backless benches called ta 榻. Those made with back rests and arm rests are called luohan chuang 罗汉床. There are 4 types of gui, namely jia ge 架格 (for the storage of books), liang ge 亮格 (closed book shelves), yuan jiao 圆角 and fang jiao gui 方角柜 (cupboards). There are 4 types of yi namely kao bei yi 靠背椅 (with back rest but no arm rest), fu shou yi 扶手椅 (with arm rest), yuan yi 圆椅 (with rounded back rest and jiao yi 交椅 (with back rest). Deng (stool) may be rectangular or square. Jue may be round, square or rectangular. An ancestor worship table is usually elaborately profiled with 4 elegantly carved legs. Besides the above mentioned types of furniture there are many miscellaneous items such as screens and boxes. The screen is called ping feng 屏风 which varies from the elaborately carved to the simply framed. A popular box for the storage of paintings and valuable items is the men xin gui 闷心柜 made of camphor wood.

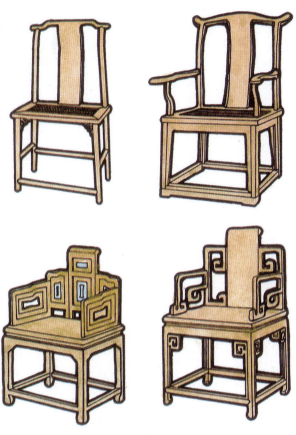

Chairs of the Ming period.

Chairs of the Qing period.

Chair arm rests can be designed in many forms. The designs shown are:

yuan bei wan shou 元背湾手 *(round), hua jie shou* 花结手*(flower), yuan tou shou* 圆头手 *(round), wei ding zhong* 尾顶中*(bell), yuan gu diao shou* 元骨钓手 *(bone) and ma an ding jie shou* 马案顶结手 *(composite).*

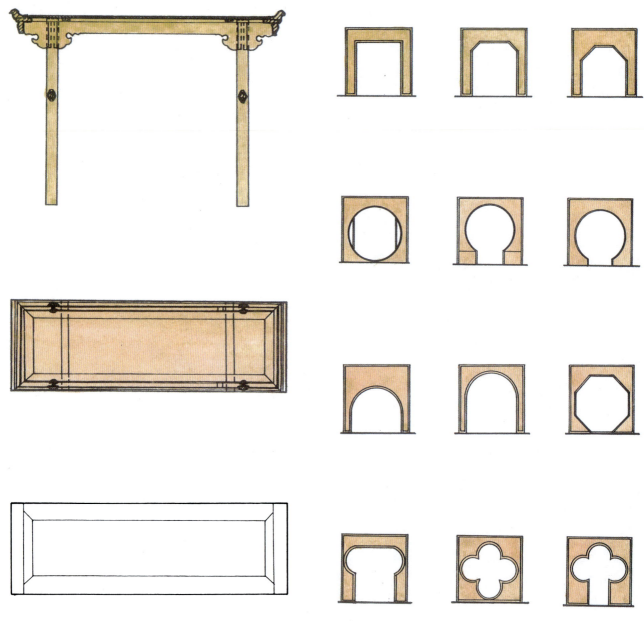

Plans and section of an altar table.

Various types of partition screens.

Imperial chair and pingfeng 屏风 *(screen) painted by author.*

Part of the beauty of Chinese cabinets and wardrobe is in the design of the metal mounts. Various forms of mount give Chinese cabinets a final touch of exquisite beauty. Patterns are engraved on the locks and handles as symbols of good fortune, fertility and longevity. Birds, animals, fish, dragons, deer, cranes and even tigers are some of the popular themes engraved on metal mounts. Ancient metal mounts were made of pai tong 白铜 (a copper-nickel-zinc alloy). Later mounts were made of brass or bronze.

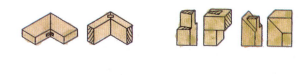

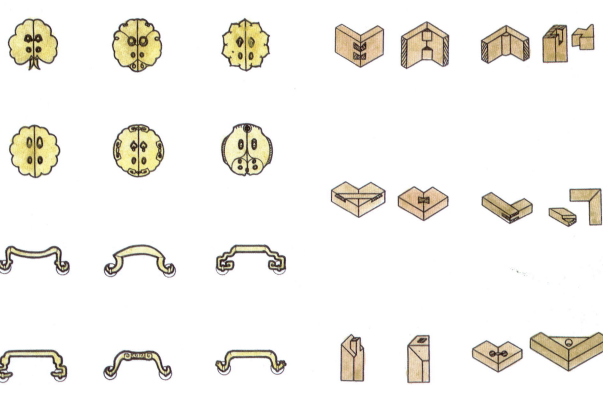

Classical design of metal mounts.

Furniture joinery.

Chinese table tops may take various shapes and forms. Eight examples are shown:
gui su 龟缩 (tortoise), *kui fan* 葵返 (square with edge), *shan mian* 扇面 (fan), *yuan* 圆 (round), *dou fang* 斗方 (square), *ri zi* 日字 (like the word ri or day), *hai tang* 海棠 (flower) and *ban yue* 半月 (half moon).

diao zhong heng 吊钟横 (bells).

diao zhu heng 吊珠横 (pearls).

yang hua heng 洋花横 (flowers).

zhu hua heng 竹花横 (bamboo).
Various types of table edge.

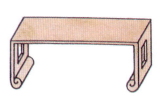

Various types of tables.

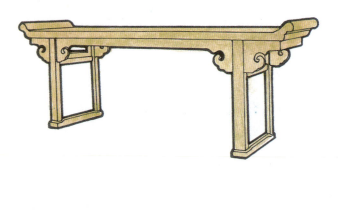

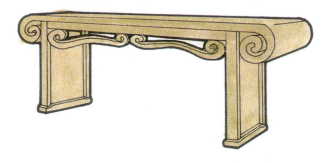

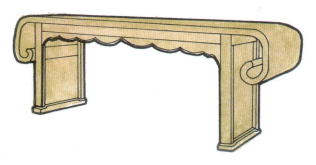

The styles of table
The edge of a table can be designed in tiers. A table can have as many as 7 tiers. The drawings above show tables carved with intricate design and style named qiao tou 翘头 *and juan tou* 卷头.

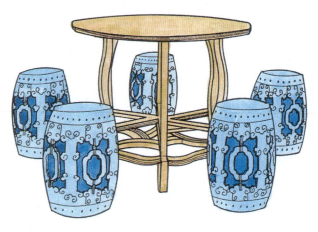

Round table with porcelain stools.

Chinese characters of good omen are stylised into harmonious patterns and engraved into the wood for making the back rests, arm rests and furniture supports. Animals, birds and plants are also stylised and engraved on furniture for decorative purposes. Some of the Chinese characters used are given in a chart as shown in the following pages.

Chinese furniture layout is based on balance and symmetry. Excellent examples of balanced layouts are found in the formal imperial palaces in the Forbidden City, Beijing. The placement of beds is made with reference to the horoscopes of the users. Each piece of furniture is a piece of art to be looked at and appreciated. Its proportion, texture, craftmanship and decorative motifs play important roles in the entire composition.

Chinese character		Meaning	Symbolism
ren	人	many people	posterity
kou	口	many mouths	posterity
ding	丁	many descendents	posterity
shou	寿	length of life	longevity
xi	喜	happy	happiness
fu	福	luck	luck
lu	禄	wealth	wealth
chun	春	spring	youthfulness
ji	吉	good	wellbeing
xiang	祥	peace	peace
sheng	升	rise	promotion
long	龙	dragon	vigour
ma	马	horse	vitality
feng	凤	phoenix	graciousness

Chinese character in Chinese writing	in pin yin	items or being equivalent to the Chinese character in terms of symbolism	meaning and significance
囍	Xi	鹊 (que, a bird)	means double happiness, often carved on furniture for newly-weds
福	Fu	蝠 (fu, a bat)	symbolises luck, carved on the back rest of armchairs and screens
寿	Shou	寿星 (shou xing, an old man)	means longevity, carved on the back rest of armchairs and on edges of supports of beds
吉	Ji	橘 (ju, a fruit)	means lucky and propitious, carved on the back rest of arm chairs
如	Ru	鱼 (yu, a fish)	means success, carved on household furniture
祝	Zhu	竹 (zhu, bamboo)	means good wishes, occasionally carved on furniture to symbolise youthfulness and auspiciousness

Patterns are carved on furniture to represent auspicious and propitious messages. These patterns usually have names similar to those Chinese characters that mean good luck.

Wisdom is represented, by the elephant while the vase 瓶 is equivalent to peace 平 ("ping" in pin yin)

Pine tree represents longevity and endurance

The dragon symbolises the yang force and the phoenix the yin. Together they represent the perfect balance of yin and yang.

Fish scales represent success.

The fish symbolises success and surplus.

The lotus represents endurance and uprightness.

Water ripples mean wealth and heavenly blessing.

Clouds represent heavenly blessing and wisdom.

Gold pieces symbolise wealth.

The qi lin 麒麟 symbolises wisdom.

Yuan yang (鸳鸯) represent the union of woman and man.

Flowers symbolise wealth.

Tortoise shells represent longevity.

The eight symbols of the eight immortals represent longevity.

Old coins represent wealth.

Bats symbolise luck.

---

5  Chinese arts

锦 瑟
jǐn   sè

李 商 隐
lǐ shāng yǐn

锦	瑟	无	端	五	十	弦，
jǐn	sè	wú	duān	wǔ	shí	xián
一	弦	一	柱	思	华	年。
yī	xián	yī	zhù	sī	huá	nián
庄	生	晓	梦	迷	蝴	蝶，
zhuāng	shēng	xiǎo	mèng	mí	hú	dié
望	帝	春	心	托	杜	鹃。
wàng	dì	chūn	xīn	tuō	dù	juān
沧	海	月	明	珠	有	泪，
cāng	hǎi	yuè	míng	zhū	yǒu	lèi
蓝	田	日	暖	玉	生	烟。
lán	tián	rì	nuǎn	yù	shēng	yān
此	情	可	待	成	追	忆，
cǐ	qíng	kě	dài	chéng	zhuī	yì
只	是	当	时	已	惘	然！
zhǐ	shì	dāng	shí	yǐ	wǎng	rán

This poem by Li Shang Yin was written about the Chinese zither of 50 strings and how each string evokes the memory of the past cherished by the poet.

CONTENTS

103

The established forms of art include disciplines as diverse as cave painting, dancing, movie making, magic performance, chess playing, pottery making, embroidery work, kite making, and fan making. However, only those that are still popular with overseas Chinese will be discussed in the sections which follow.

5.1 | Introduction

China's rich historical past is vividly expressed in her colourful achievements in the various art forms. As early as several hundred years before the Zhou dynasty hundreds of poetic songs were created for entertainment and ritual. The development of poetic writings flourished through successive dynasties, and by the Tang period many noted poets such as Li Bai 李白 and Bai Juyi 白居易 were recognised for their creative and poetic writings. As early as the Shang period paintings on the walls of the imperial palaces were executed to record the achievements of the feudal lords. Arts of many forms were closely related to politics and religion. Almost four thousand years ago Chinese calligraphy and writing on pottery, tortoise shells and bronzeware were evident. The Chinese traditions of dance and opera were created before the Chunqiu period as recorded in the Lushi Chunqiu 吕氏春秋. The art of cooking developed so early that by the Zhou dynasty there were as many as 130 recipes on the cooking of vegetables and 200 on meat, and now there are countless styles and varieties of Chinese cuisine.

5.2 | Calligraphy

Calligraphy, the art of writing with a brush, is deeply rooted in Chinese culture, and can be traced back almost 4,000 years. While it is not within the scope of this book to teach the art itself, a brief introduction will encourage those interested in proceeding to further study.

Chinese calligraphic characters showing the various forms of writing: kai, xing, cao, li and do zhuan.

The first and oldest writings were engraved on tortoise shells and date back as far as the Shang Dynasty (1711–1066 BC). These writings can be traced back to their inventor, Cang Xie, who was an official of Huang Di, the ancient emperor. The shells first appeared at Henan, Anyang but they were made widely known only in 1899 during the Qing dynasty.

A style of writing found on bone inscriptions from the Chunqiu Warring States period (722–481 BC) was invented by Zhou 籀, an official of the Zhou court, and named Zhou Wen after the Zhou dynasty. It was also known as da zhuan 大篆 or big seal script. Li Si 李斯, a prime minister of the Qin emperor (221–206 BC) created the xiao zhuan 小篆 or

These words were part of the 204 engraved imprint on steles dating back to the Qin era. The writing style was based on the zhuan shu 篆书.

This phrase "Kao nian li zi" 考年立子 (literally:examine year establish son) is classified as yin jia gu wen 殷甲骨文 which is the zhuan style 篆书 of Han writing.

The words "deng yu fengshan" 登于峰山 (reaching the feng hill) were copied from a plaque dating back to Qin Shi Huang Di.

small seal script, which was based on the da zhuan. Li Si was a shrewd politician who served the first emperor, Qin Shi Huang Di 秦始皇帝, and worked his way up to become prime minister. He was instrumental in the destruction and burning of old classics and literary works during the rule of the Qin emperor. He helped Zhao Gao 赵高, who was originally from the Zhao state but after having served the Qin emperor for over 20 years became a trusted and powerful figure in Qin politics. Zhao was infamous for having plotted against the eldest son of Qin Shi Huang Di in 209 BC and presented a false document, supposedly the will of the deceased Qin emperor, to declare the second son, who was in his complete control, the legal successor.

Zhao Gao was noted for his contribution to the advancement of calligraphic skill and bequeathed us his style of writing in Taishan, a book of calligraphy based on the xiao zhuan style. The zhuan are written as rounded characters of consistent thickness with curved tracks. In the Han dynasty (206 BC–220 AD) a style of writing with bold-faced tracks and neat characters made up of square and curved lines, named old dishu 棣书, was created by Cheng Miao 程邈 while he was imprisoned. It was later popularised and it evolved to become the new dishu from which modern styles of writing such as caoshu 草书, zhengkai 正楷 and xingshu 行书 were developed.

During the Han period two noted calligraphers, Cui Ai 崔瑗 and Du Du 杜度 practised the caoshu and earned themselves fame and re-

This phrase "Qing tou zhi he" 情投志合 (compatible and sharing same aspirations) was modeled on di shu.

These words "feng yu" 风雨 *(wind and water) were modeled on di* 棣书.

spect. A disciple of Cui Ai named Zhang Zhi 张芝 became famous for his caoshu calligraphy and his very own style which was regarded as caosheng 草圣 (the best of caoshu). An East Jin calligrapher, Wang Xi Zhi 王羲之 (321–379 AD), who learnt the kaishu and caoshu from such great masters as Zhang Zhi, 张芝 formalised the xiao zhuan script and made it look more distinctive. Then a style between the lishu and caoshu was created by Liu De Sheng 刘德昇. During the Tang dynasty China's art and architecture flourished, and Zhang Xu 张旭, a calligrapher noted for his kaishu and caoshu, created a refreshing new style. He was known to be most creative when he was drunk. He screamed and dribbled wine as he wrote briskly and continuously.

The differences between the text style, kaishu, and the cursive style, caoshu, are that the former consists of structured and squarish characters while the latter consists of curved, elongated and free-flowing characters. The

This phrase "fan shu dui ke you hao qi" 饭蔬对客有豪气 *(It is generous to offer rice and vegetables to the guests) was first written by Ming dynasty calligraphers using caoshu* 草 *This phrase was demonstrated in Ling Yun Chao's calligraphy.*

弟子王逸少甚能學衛真書

This phrase "di zi Wang Yi Shao shen neng xue wei zhen shu" 弟子王逸少能 学卫真书 (Can I, Wang Yi Shao learn from the Book of Truth) is taken from Madam Jin's Kaishu 楷书.

calligrapher has certain rules to follow depending on the style of calligraphy he practises. For the text style he has to hold the brush firmly at a lower point. For the cursive style the brush has to be held high and its movement should be free and intuitive, expressing the life in the characters. The advantage of the cursive style is that the calligrapher can use symbols and omit parts of the writing without changing the original meaning. However, in both styles the character is formed with the same basic stroke — pushing, pulling, dragging or moving the brush to form light or hard, vertical or horizontal, dotted or circling lines.

There are as many as 28 types of calligraphic strokes. Twenty of them are mentioned in Zeng Qiao's records on Chinese history published as Tong Zhi. Zeng Qiao (1103–1162 AD) was a scholar and writer of the Southern Song era. He was an expert on the study of geography, astronomy and herbs. Another scholar, Jiang Shan Guo 蒋善国, introduced 8 types of stroke which form the basis of Chinese calligraphic types, ranging from the seal script to the text script.

Chinese calligraphy and the way the character is written is closely linked to Chinese symbolism. One of the oldest classical records of the characters, Shuowen 说文, dated 121 AD, has a record of 9,000 characters and gives an insight into the original Chinese symbolism in the written form. Many Chinese words were created from gestures, man-made models and other things related to man. For example, the word ming 名 (name) was formed by the characters xi 夕 (night) and kou 口 (mouth). This could have been because while in broad daylight there was no need to ask the name of a person approaching, at night one is not able to see clearly and so has to open one's mouth and ask the person to identify himself. Thus, the identity or name was written as ming 名 (a character made up of xi 夕 and kou 口). Some words that have their origins in pictorial models, actual forms of living things and natural phenomenona, are listed below:

Written characters		meaning	origins depicted pictorially
fu	夫	husband	木
shou	手	hand	乎
er	耳	ear	巪
shan	山	hills	山
shui	水	water	川
yang	羊	goat	羊
niu	牛	ox	半
ma	马	horse	馬
tian	田	padi	田

Sometimes Chinese characters may be repeated to reinforce their significance and form a new character. For example, the word mu 木 (wood or tree) may be written twice to mean lin 林 (woods with many trees) or three times to mean sen 森 (a thick forest). The word xin 心 (heart) was derived from the picture of a heart and many words that are related to man's emotions are written with the word xin as a radical. Some of these words are: ren 忍 (to suppress emotion), yuan 怨 (to blame), shu 恕 (to forgive), xiang 想 (to think of), chou 愁 (to feel unhappy), ci 慈 (to feel compassionate for), wei 慰 (to comfort), and gan 感 (to feel).

Every completed piece of calligraphic work is stamped with a seal with the name of the calligrapher, for identification purposes. Sometimes a piece of calligraphy bears more than one seal because some seals contain words of greeting, propitious sayings or attributes. Some ancient calligraphic writings bear the collectors' seals as well. Words carved in the seals may be stylised for artistic effect and the engraving may be in relief (yang seal) or in intaglio (yin seal).

5.3 | Brush painting

In the old days there was little difference between a Chinese calligrapher and a brush painter. A calligrapher was trained to write with the brush from a tender age and so he could handle the brush and control the water using them as effective means of expressing space, form and structure in his calligraphy. Brush painting was very similar to calligraphy as the artist used the basic calligraphic brush strokes in painting. Both forms of art portrayed the structure and form of the brush strokes and were performed with the same tools.

An early painting dating back to the 4th century BC was recently discovered at Changsha. From historical records it was learnt that during the Han dynasty (206 BC–220 AD) there were court artists serving the emperors to promote brush painting. By the Jin period (265–420 AD) the portraits were skilfully painted with a brush. During the Sui dynasty (581–618 AD) the art of brush painting flourished and artists such as Zhan Zi Qian 展子虔 and Dong Bo Ren 董伯仁 were well versed in landscape and figure painting.

The arts continued to flourish during the Tang period (618–907 AD). Great masters of brush painting included Wu Dao Zi 吴道子, Wang Wei 王维, Li Cheng Xun 李成训 and Zhou Fang 周纺. Brush painting continued to develop during the Five Dynasties (907–960 AD) and the Song period (960–1279 AD). Landscape and other types of painting reached a high standard as arts centres established themselves and grew. The art centres enjoyed the patronage of the emperors. Accomplished artists were offered posts in the imperial courts, and the emperor himself was an accomplished painter.

When the Yuan dynasty was established the Chinese arts centres were not supported by the rulers. Artists were not discouraged however, but persevered to achieve greater excellence in their disciplines. Some noted artists were Zhu De Run 朱德润, Kang Di 康棣, Huang Gong Wang 黄公望, Wu Zheng 吴镇, Wang Meng 王蒙, Ni Zan 倪赞 and they were totally dedicated to bringing the standard of brush painting to a higher plane.

Although the Ming rulers (1368–1644 AD) tried to bring back the glory and the high standards of the Tang dynasty in the arts centres it was not an easy task. The Ming rulers such as Xun De 宣德 (1426–1435 AD) were

Carps by author.

devoted to promoting brush painting. Some noted and talented artists, Shen Zhou 沈周, Wen Zheng Ming 文徵明, Tang Yin 唐寅 and Chou Ying 仇英 created outstanding masterpieces and a style of their own.

By the time of the Qing dynasty tremendous achievements had been made by painters. Landscape artists included Shi Tao 石涛, Mei Qing 梅青 and the Eight Eccentrics. The emperor Qian Long 乾隆 was himself a patron and master brush painter. He specialised in flowers, birds and landscapes. Later artists such as Zhao Zhi Qian 赵之谦, Wu Chang Shuo 吴昌硕, Qi Bai Shi 齐白石 and Ren Bai Nian 任伯年 produced the most creative and skilful works.

Like calligraphic work Chinese brush painting is stamped with a seal, usually in a place that enhances the balance of the painting. The seal is often placed after the name of the painter at the end of a written phrase, philosophical verse or poem that compliments the painting. Sometimes several seals are found on a painting because the collectors or calligraphers other than the artist wish to leave their own imprints on the painting.

5.3.1 | Media used for Chinese brush paintings

The essential items needed for Chinese brush painting are the brush, the ink, the ink stone and rice paper or silk. Colours are optional because an effective or traditional Chinese brush painting is not necessarily finished in colour. In ancient times most paintings were monochromatic.

THE BRUSH

The brushwork in a Chinese painting is the most important element because it is the "backbone" and "lifenerve" of the painting. Therefore, the choice and the use of the brushes are carefully considered to achieve the desired result for the type of painting. Brushes are made from various types of animal hair such as goat's, wolf's, leopard's, horse's, pig's or rabbit's hair. Usually they are made in factories where the hair or fibres are bound, cemented and punched into a brush with hair lengths ranging from long to short, building

A Chinese brush painting is not complete without the name and the seal of the author of the painting. This photograph shows the author putting her seal on her painting.

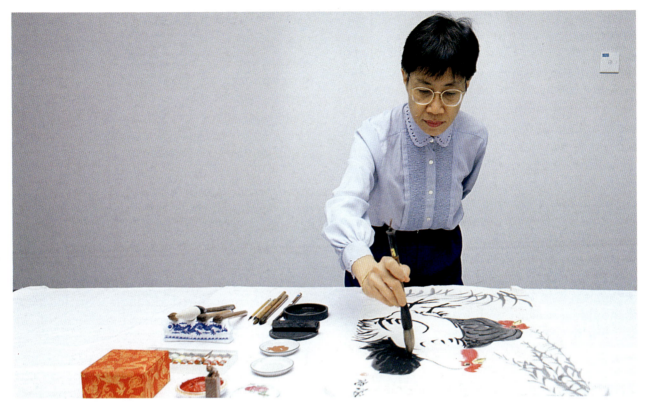

The author painting roosters on rice papers.
The photograph shows the author using a big brush to paint roosters. In the picture some brushes of various sizes,
a seal and some colours can be seen.

up to a tip. Chinese brushes are made in various sizes and qualities. Those made of goat hair are softer than those made of wolf or rabbit hair.

The history of Chinese brushmaking can be traced back almost 4,000 years to when the brush was used for writing and the expression of artistic symbols. This was the case not only in China but also in the western world. For example, while simple cave paintings in Spain and France and tomb paintings in Egypt were being painted with rudimentary brushes, delicate paintings incorporating detail such as birds' feathers were painted with a Chinese brush in China.

Nowadays, many types of Chinese brushes can be purchased. The price of a brush depends on its quality and size (in Singapore a goat-hair brush may cost only a few dollars but a sizable wolf-hair brush may cost as much as $30). Although the artist may prefer the firmness of wolf or rabbit hair brushes, those made of goat's hair are more refined, softer and can hold more water.

The hair of the Chinese brush is flexible but the use of the brush is a difficult skill to master. In using the brush the artist has to control the speed of application. He should be fast and yet his brush should not piao 飘 or drift. But if he wishes to make some slow strokes with his brush he should avoid blotting. Lines or strokes made by the brush should vary from xu shi 虚实 (light and hard, thin and thick or wet and dry strokes). The brush should have a tip and it should be used with appropriate pressure, spacing and consistency. When a brush is new it should be dipped in cold water for some time before it is used with ink. After it has been used it should be washed with soap and clean water and left to dry on a brush rack.

THE INK

The ink stick is usually made of pine resin or tong oil burnt beneath a hood to produce a residue which is then mixed into a solution with glue. This mixture is dried in rectangular or round sticks. The manufacturing process and materials used determine the quality, colour, texture, smell and price of the ink stick.

Chinese ink may be bought either in solid (stick) or liquid form. Artists prefer to grind the ink stick on their own ink stone for quality art work. Some collect all forms of ink sticks which may be made so exquisitely that they are works of art in themselves.

THE INK STONE

The ink stone is a utensil for grinding and holding ink. The materials for the manufacture of ink stones are now limited to stone and earthenware. In the past other materials such as steel, jade, silver and copper had been used. The design of such ink utensils could be exquisitely cast or carved.

The quality of an ink stone is obvious through the examination of the colour, texture of the stone and how well it absorbs water (the smoother the texture the better the quality). Slightly greenish stone is believed to be less absorbent and is of a higher quality. The technique and art of grinding the ink stick on the stone is acquired through experience. A slow and consistent circular movement of the wrist, applying even pressure while grinding the ink stick on the stone is believed to produce the finest quality ink liquid. Water on the stone is supposed to be added little by little while grinding. It is important to keep the stone clean and so it should be washed after use and kept clean.

THE PAPER AND SILK

Chinese brush painting may be applied on ceramics, lacquer works, silk rice paper. The use of silk for Chinese brush painting was introduced as early as the Zhou dynasty (1122–256 BC). Rice paper was not used until Cai Lun 蔡伦 invented the technique of paper making in 105 AD, during the Han dynasty. The method of rice paper making improved and so refinement and variety developed. By the Tang dynasty rice paper had become a popular medium for scroll painting.

Rice paper is made from cotton, the bark of trees or bamboo. That made from cotton or bamboo is fairly absorbent and suitable for the quick technique while that which has been processed with glue is non-absorbent and good for detailed paintings. Numerous varieties, sizes and qualities of paper are available to the artist.

THE COLOURS

During the early period the only colours used on Chinese brush painting were different shades of black ink. An accomplished artist was able to show seven shades of ink on a monochromatic painting. When colours were first introduced they were made from natural stone. Presently, watercolours made from vegetable and mineral materials are commonly applied on Chinese scrolls. Blue is derived from the mineral azurite, green from malachite and red from cinnabar or iron oxide.

THE SEALS

The purpose of the seal is to certify authorship and ownership. In the past the owners of noted Chinese brush paintings used to endorse their ownership of the paintings through the imprint of their seals. Sometimes an old painting is valued more highly because it bears the seals of many well-known past owners.

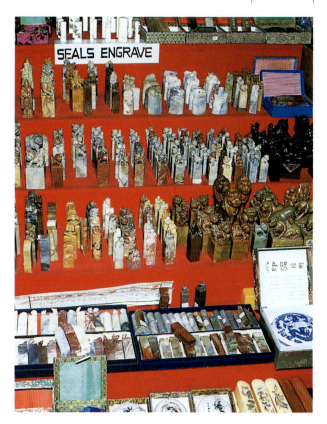

Chinese seals may be carved with stones or ivory or jade.

The success in the design of the seal lies in the balance and harmony of the linework and spatial composition created by the seal carver. The shapes of seals may vary from square to round. A few examples of carved seals are shown below to illustrate the artistic composition of lines and space. A seal is applied with a waxy oil based ink made from powdered cinnabar. The characters of the name of the owner are carved and engraved on the seal which may be made of stone or ivory.

Yang seal Sheng Dan Kuai Le 圣诞快乐 *(Merry Christmas) by Koh Thong Ngee.*
The characters in this seal, based on the Zhuan Shu 篆书 *are yang wen* 阳文 *(positive characters) and will appear in red. Note how well balanced the seal is.*

Yin seal Jiang Shan Duo Jiao 江山多娇 *by Koh Thong Ngee.*
This bodly carved seal based on the Li Shu 隶书 *balances the masculine characters in a forceful composition.*

Yang seal Gong He Xin Xi 恭贺新禧 *by Koh Thong Ngee.*
The yang seal above can be compared to this bolder seal containing good wishes for Chinese New Year.

Yang seal Mei Yi Yan Nian 美意延年 *by Koh Thong Ngee.*
This seal captures the essence of the art of seal carving. Lively lines divide the composition into spaces, each pleasingly different from the others. The entire composition is rhythmic, perfectly balanced and gives a terrific sense of space.

Yang seal Xin Ru 心如 : by Koh Thong Ngee.
This seal is an excellent example of how interest and
significance can be created by symbols. The message
conveyed by the two characters xin ru (follow the
heart) is Daoist in essence, but when ru Is placed
above xin the character created is shu (forgive)
which is a Confucian sentiment. Note how the xin
character resembles the shape of a man's heart.

Yin seal The Romance of the Three Kingdoms by Koh
Thong Ngee.
This yin seal truly shows the skill of the artist as it
reminisces about the changing tides in politics and the
heroes of the Three Kingdoms Era. The characters
engraved on the irregularly-shaped stone read:
Successes and failures of the heroes are compared to
the flow of the river Jiang - eventually all will come
to nothing. No matter how tides and fortunes change,
the country and the natural world will remain the
same.

5.3.2 | Chinese brush painting techniques

INTRODUCTION

Chinese brush painting technique has its limitations in terms of method of application and medium of presentation. But once the technique is grasped it is a most delightful means of conveying creative and artistic expression on paper. As modification of the painting is not possible the inspiration of the artist is expressed intuitively and permanently the moment the brush strokes have been made. The brush painter, therefore, has to master the double task of creating and demonstrating his ideas instantaneously on paper.

As mentioned in the introduction, there are two schools of painting — the intuitive (also known as lineless) and the detailed approach (line painting). The former is more difficult to master with distinction. The merest hint of an outline of the object in the painting is to be avoided. The artist has to apply the intuitive technique and skill that he has acquired over the years to demonstrate his ability to control the medium and his artistic expression. He has to show his confidence and skill through spontaneous ease in his application of brush strokes on the rice paper. The line or detailed painting requires the painter to be patient and to study the object or objects of the painting carefully so that the texture, the shape, and the composition will be captured in ink on rice paper. The details and textures are portrayed with lines of brushwork, then ink

Brush painting of a boy and a dog by author.

washes are added before colours are finally applied.

It is recommended that students of Chinese brush painting take up the art of calligraphy in order to master the control of a brush and the use of the ink and paper. After they have done this they should study the line or detailed painting technique to learn the skill of capturing the details of the natural world without which it is difficult for them to imagine or portray the spirits of things in nature. Very often, in schools of Chinese brush painting the students are first asked to copy and reproduce the works of old masters in order to acquire basic skills and techniques which will be of great help to them when they embark on the lineless style of painting. They learn from the established styles, albeit through imitation, unconsciously acquiring the techniques by which they will subsequently express their own ideas. Only after they have learnt how to capture the details of an object or a landscape will they be able to express their essence in spontaneous strokes of the brush.

A successful Chinese brush painter not only has complete control of his brush but also knows how to maximise the usage of the medium. If the brush holds too much ink, blots may form. But if it does not hold enough ink it shows insufficient "qi yun" (resonance). The flow of ink should be fluent and firm. Therefore, the structural use of the brush and the understanding of the mediums of painting must be grasped before the technique of forming interesting composition in a painting is mastered.

The application of colours should be mastered to give lustre and reinforce the work. It should be used to bring out light and shade, vigour and movement as well as the beauty of nature.

In composition, the artist should aim at creating space and resonance. He should not try to fill the entire piece of rice paper with paint but to achieve the strongest contrast between the essential and inessential. If a painting of black ink is on a white background the latter itself should be a part of the entire composition. It is also important to render the painting a sense of perspective in the composition. For example, the hills in the foreground are painted with clefts and ridges while those far away are not. The rivers in the foreground have ripples but those far away do not. The composition should show life and dynamic movement. Mountains and rivers may twist and turn portraying power and vigour. Haste and confusion, as well as over-crowding and disorder in composition must be avoided.

PAINTING FLOWERS, FRUITS AND PLANTS

A student should master the various brush strokes such as dian 点 (dots), heng 橫 (horizontal strokes) and jian 尖 (vertical strokes) before attempting a painting. The dian stroke is made by holding the brush straight and upright and barely letting the tip of the brush touch the paper, to make a dot. Heng strokes are made by turning the brush in a horizontal direction while jian strokes can be made in a vertical direction.

Learning the technique of painting of flowers, fruits and plants is made easier when one studies them first in their natural state. The artist should sketch them and make close observations of their characteristics and forms and their colours and textures. The artist may start painting them in a "line" painting and sketch them with the brush again and again to portray them from different angles and in perspective as well as at different stages of growth.

Once the artist has grasped the spirit, and external appearance of the flowers, fruits and plants he can then paint them in the "lineless" or intuitive style, bearing in mind the following:

1) The picture should be clearly formulated in his mind before he executes the painting.
2) He should paint the flowers and plants with vigour and spirit. His brush strokes should be applied more with intuition than hesitation.
3) He should portray the branches, leaves and other parts with "life" and strength and in different positions. The blossoms or fruits, may be at different stages of growth and should also be painted in a variety of positions.

Popular flowers that have explicit symbolic implications are plum blossom, the orchid, the chrysanthemum and the bamboo. These flowers and plants represent longevity and endurance.

Plum blossom is one of the most colourful flowers and is expressed as five red petals. It is important to paint the trunk first, and the

Intuitive painting of roosters.

Chrysanthemum.

flowers in dots of pink in various positions. Sometimes the white blossom is outlined in ink to indicate purity. The stamens and the dotted pollen are then added.

Orchids are to be painted with life and character as they represent uprightness and endurance. Their leaves are long and elegant but should be painted with a single stroke. Leaves may crisscross in various positions to form an interesting and natural composition.

The chrysanthemum is described along with the orchid, the plum and the bamboo as one of the "si junzi" 四君子 (the four cultured gen-

A brush painting of trees and rocks done on rice paper.

Lotus by author.

tlemen) and is the brightest of them all. It is painted yellow, giving much vigour and life to a scroll.

The evergreen bamboo is a symbol of longevity, and is popular among scholars as a subject for demonstrating their skill in handling the brush. The first step is to paint the bamboo canes or branches. The section near the roots or at the top has shorter segments, and the parts in the middle have longer segments. At the fifth segment branches grow out of the main cane. Leaves in black ink are then added to the plant in different positions.

The lotus is another flower which is popular with brush painters. It grows out of the muddy pond and rises up in a dignified posture signifying uprightness, beauty and purity.

The lotus is a large flower with sizeable petals and leaves and so large brushes are used to paint them. A lotus flower in full bloom may have many petals and its leaves may be as large as a metre in diameter. Before starting to paint, the artist should imagine the entire composition and define the spirit of the painting. The leaves should be painted first, using a large brush. The form and structure of the leaves can be portrayed through the use of dark and light dashes of ink. The veins of the leaves can be added later. The stems may be as long as two metres in reality and they must be painted with strength and vigour in one continuous stroke. The thorns are painted when the stems are almost dry with quick strokes of the brush. Lotus flowers are painted either in outline or with the tip of a large brush forming the petals. The brush should contain just sufficient water tinged with a light red. The tip of the brush should be dipped in a much darker red so that when the petals of the flower are painted the tips of the petals look darker than the rest of the petals. Buds of the lotus are painted using the same technique.

This shows the author singing Chinese opera in an Arts festival. Note the background and backdrop were made up of cardboards painted with lotus.

When attempting to paint a fruit it is best to start by placing the fruit on a table and make sketches of it. Having carefully studied the characteristics of different fruits the student can then paint them more vividly. For example, when painting a bunch of rambutans, he would first paint the shape of the fruit and then add the hair and the branches and leaves.

Painting vegetables is similar to painting fruit in the sense that the composition, the way the vegetables are grouped and the contrast of their colours, textures and shapes, is very important.

LANDSCAPE PAINTING

Landscape painting is an excellent form of scroll painting. It is essential for the landscape artist to grasp the "qi" 气 and "shen" 神 of the mountains, clouds, trees, plants, rocks, sand, rapid mist and water, and translate the essence of these elements onto the paper with vivid realism and breath of life. The artist should aim to form interesting compositions in the landscape scroll showing a sense of perspective and depicting natural beauty.

The principles applying to landscape painting are known as "shan shui hua" 山水画. These state that there must be a strong contrast of dark and light elements using shades of ink ranging from very dark to very light.

The formation of the physical features such as rugged mountains, rocks and trees as seen in their natural state should be shown with bold strokes of the brush. The colours are built up by the layer upon layer method. Waterfalls and rivers should have sources and rockeries should be three-dimensional. All natural elements such as trees and plants must be natural and well-formed.

The composition should not be over-crowded, and stiffness is to be avoided. Even though the landscape painting should be a true likeness as far as possible, the spirit and the structure of the painting are considerations which are as important as other aspects of the painting. There should be ample contrast between the yin and yang elements in the painting. For example, the rugged shaded sides of the mountains should be contrasted with the smooth areas in the sunlight. The high mountains should be balanced by deep valleys. The barks of twisted old pine trees may be brought to life by green lichen and twigs entwined. In a well-executed monochromatic, vigorous and lively landscape painting there may be as many as 9 shades of black.

Besides contrast there must be harmony and beauty in a landscape painting. The skill of achieving harmony is even more challenging than that of creating contrast. In using dark and light shades of ink to create interesting forms the artist must ensure that they are in a harmonious composition.

PAINTING BIRDS AND CHICKS

The basic approach to painting birds and chicks is similar to landscape and flower painting as described earlier. In order to paint a bird or a chick the artist must have studied the bird carefully and observed its structure, posture,

Landscape painting by author.

movement and habits of feeding. To capture the spirit and movement of a bird the artist must apply his brush strokes spontaneously and without interruption on paper. The steps involved in the execution of the painting of a bird can be summarised as follows:

1) The beaks are to be painted in outline with a couple of quick but decisive strokes. The eyes are then added.
2) The head of the bird is formed with a single stroke of the brush.
3) The back portion is painted with another stroke.
4) The breast is usually a light shade.
5) The tail is dark.
6) The wings are added with very dark ink strokes.
7) Movements of the bird are expressed by the addition of the legs and claws.
8) Colours, if desirable, are added at the end.

To paint chicks, hens and cocks the artist must first make close study of their physical structure and appearance. Before he embarks on painting them he must formulate the entire composition in his mind with regard to the posture, movement and spirit of the fowls and how they relate to the other elements in the painting. A fully grown cock is covered with feathers and it has a beak, eyes, a red upper and lower crown, ears, a breast, a back, a waist, a stomach, legs and claws. To paint a cock or a chick these steps should be followed:

1) Paint the beak first.
2) Add the eyes and then the crown with one bold stroke of the brush (the crown of a small chick is small)

A brush painting of fish in a lotus pond done on rice paper.

Chinese brush painting of chicks by the author.

3) Paint the back with another stroke.
4) The breast is painted a light shade.
5) The wings are added with a dark dash of ink.

5.4 | Music

Musical instruments and musical notation were well developed as early as the Zhou dynasty (1122–249 BC). Numerous types of musical instruments such as the zhong 钟, the gu 鼓, the xun 埙, the hao 号, the di 笛 and the kong 箜 were invented to compliment dances, songs and dramas. The zhong, a green copper instrument hung and beaten to make musical notes, was made as early as the Western Zhou period (1066–256 BC). Pian zhong, a group of bell-like copper instruments hanging from a wooden frame, were made for imperial court entertainment. During the Qin dynasty (221–206 BC) the pi pa 琵琶 was popularly used. As early as the Warring States (3rd century AD) in the State of Qin stringed instruments mounted on rectangular boxes called sun 箕 were made to accompany songs and dramas. During the reign of Han Wu Di 汉武帝 a harp-like stringed instrument called kong hou 箜篌 was invented by Hou Diao 候调. From the Han (206 BC–220 AD) to the Sui (589–618 AD) many musical instruments such as the gu (a drum), the xun (a porcelain instrument for harmonious sound), the hao (a bamboo instrument with long and short sections), the di (a bamboo horizontal flute), the flute and others were made. The most notable of the promoters of music and drama during the

Sui dynasty were Niu Hong 牛弘, He An 何安 and the emperor, Sui Yang Di 隋阳帝 (569–618 AD), who was a gifted musician himself.

The development of musical instruments and notation carried on into the Tang dynasty (618–907 AD). Among the patrons was the emperor himself. Emperor Tang Tai Zong 唐太宗 (599–649 AD) ascended to the throne in 626 AD and he tried to improve the economy of the country, and using himself as a model, he also encouraged musicians to develop the skill of using musical instruments. Others such as Lu Cai 吕才 (600–665 AD), a philosopher on the theory of yin and yang, and Li Bai Yao 李百药 (565–648 AD) a historian and author of books on etiquette, also helped to revive classical music and bring it to further heights.

5.5 | The art of tea drinking

One of the ancient Chinese arts that has certainly not been forgotten or discarded

Tea leaves in plates.

is the art of making and serving tea. This particular art is popularly practised among the common people, be they Buddhists, Daoists or Confucianists, because tea is taken not just as a means of quenching thirst and ridding the body of excessive oil, but also to nurture the spirit — yi qing yang xing 怡情养性 (to move the feelings and nurture the spirit). The making of tea and the art of serving it have been written about by many scholars through the centuries. During the Han dynasty (3rd century BC) Wang Bao 王褒 and Tong Yue 僮约 wrote the world's oldest essays on tea drinking. In the Jin period (3rd century AD) Xie An 谢安, a calligrapher, wrote on the subject of tea.

By the Tang dynasty (618–907 AD) many authors wrote on the tea ceremony and the art of making tea. Some of these authors were: Lu Tong 庐仝, Jiao Ran 皎然 and Lu Yu 陆羽. Song writers from the 10th to the 13th century included Tao Gu 陶谷, Cai Xiang 蔡襄 and Su Shi 苏轼. De Hui 德辉, a Yuan dynasty writer, was well known amongst Buddhists for his tea ceremony. Noted Ming dynasty authors included Xu Ci Shu 许次纾 and Zhou Gao Qi 周高起. By the Qing dynasty many writers, such as Wang Hao 汪灝, Chen Meng Lei 陈梦雷 and Liu Yuan Chang 刘源长, wrote on tea drinking as a form of art.

The habit of drinking tea in China started during the Zhou dynasty (1066–256 BC). The skill of making and serving tea was regarded as important as early as the Han dynasty (206 BC–220 AD). Zhu Xi 朱熹, a South Song dynasty philosopher, started the practice of drinking tea in a certain ritual and his tea ceremony was handed down and further highlighted by such scholars such as the 8th century scholar, Lu Yu 陆羽 (Tang dynasty) and Huang Ru Ze 黄儒则 (Song dynasty). Today, the tea ceremony is being revived by overseas Chinese and it is a popular cultural activity. Lu Yu wrote a book named Cha Jing 茶经 in which the origin, the production, the utensils, the making and the drinking of tea were discussed. He also popularised the art of tea drinking as he travelled widely and associated with all kinds of people ranging from scholars to businessmen. He established many tea houses to facilitate tea drinking ceremonies. Through his works the names of tea leaves, the utensils used for making tea, the materials used for boiling water and the tea houses were known to a large following of tea drinkers.

Another promoter of the art of tea drinking and author of books on the tea ceremony was Su Shi 苏轼, an expert tea maker of the Song dynasty. During that period tea makers improved the process of tea by laying down seven steps. The first was to ensure the tea leaves were picked at the right time and with the nails of the workers rather than the fingers. The second was to ensure the tea leaves were properly classified. The third was to ensure that the tea leaves were appropriately steamed. The fourth to the seventh were to ensure the making of tea was done in the best way.

By the Ming and Qing dynasty the types of tea leaves can be broadly classified into four namely ming 茗, mo zi 末子, la 蜡 and mao 毛. Ming tea consists of young tea leaves and it is drunk with the leaves. Mo zi is dried and is

Tea ceremony.
Tea should be made in careful steps. First water is heated in a glass teapot over the fire of the jiu jin lu or golden wine stove. Once the water boils it is poured into the small teapot to wash the tea leaves. The water is then poured away and more boiled water is added. After about 30 seconds the tea is served. Three cups are filled with tea even though there are only 2 people. The third cup is to enable the participants to enjoy the fragrance of the tea.

ground into powder while la consists of tea leaves made into a biscuit first before it is washed and made into tea. Mao is made from tea leaves and other fruits in little hard pieces.

The skill of tea making and drinking is expressed in seven basic steps: the preparation of the tea leaves, the preparation of the water, the starting of the fire for boiling the tea, getting the right temperature of the water for the boiling of tea leaves, putting in the tea leaves, boiling the tea leaves and serving the tea. The best type of water for high quality tea is water from the hills. Tea drinking today is usually streamlined into a simpler ceremony. It may be carried out in one of three ways, namely gai wan shi 盖碗式 (covering the cup style), cha niang shi 茶娘式 (tea and paternal style) and gong fu shi 功夫式 (skilful style). Gai wan shi is the simplest because only a tea cup with its cover are used to contain the tea and the tea drinker simply sips the tea and enjoys it. Cha niang shi is the most common and it is made in a teapot (symbolising the mother or parent) and served in cups (symbolising the children). Gong fu shi is the most authentic as it has its origin and tea ceremony from Lu Yu's treatise. The utensils used are: a heating stove, a teapot, a tea tray and some teacups, a fan, and a pair of chopsticks. First of all, the water is boiled over the porcelain stove and once it has boiled it is poured into the porcelain teapot just to wash the tea leaves. More water is boiled again and poured over the outside of the teapot and into it to make the tea.

6  Chinese opera

金缕衣
jīn lǚ yī

杜秋娘
dù qiū niáng

劝 君 莫 惜 金 缕 衣，
quàn jūn mò xī jīn lǚ yī

劝 君 惜 取 少 年 时。
quàn jūn xī qǔ shào nián shí

花 开 堪 折 直 须 折，
huā kāi kān zhé zhí xū zhé

莫 待 无 花 空 折 枝。
mò dài wú huā kōng zhé zhī

A lady named Du Qiu Niang wrote this poem during the Tang dynasty. She reminded her boyfriend to value and make the most of time and youth. Material things, like a golden coat, was not as valuable as precious time.

This poem reflects the outstanding and unusual attitude of Du Qiu Niang who did not value money and material things as other Chinese did. Her story is often depicted in Chinese opera.

CONTENTS

131

6.1 | Introduction

Chinese opera is stage drama that depicts Chinese values, aspects of life, historical events, folklore and beliefs and although it comes under the umbrella of Chinese art it merits its own section. The story upon which a Chinese opera is based usually teaches a moral lesson. Sometimes it reflects the decadence of ancient society and the weakness of man. Sometimes it preaches unity, loyalty, filial piety, righteousness or endurance.

Since Chinese opera originates from a vast country like China it has many forms such as pingxi 平戏, yuexi 粤戏 etc depending on the origin of its birth. Different regions popularise different types of play and styles of opera. Thus regional theatres use their own dialects and musical notation although they share the same techniques and themes. Themes and characters have not changed drastically over the years. Even though artists presenting a play may change completely, the story, the musical notation, the actions and gestures of each character in the play will remain the same from one production to the next. Each play usually has a climax and an ending which show that good triumphs over evil.

Lou Mee Wah in the General's role and Joanna Wong as Chen Bi Niang, the General's wife.

Chinese opera is staged not just for entertainment but also on festive occasions and, in the old days, in wealthy homes, during the mourning period after the death of an elderly member of the family. It has been handed down from generation to generation for thousands of years. It demands a great deal of devotion from the actors and actresses as it can only be grasped after years of training. It also needs an audience which understands its basic approach in terms of its artistic significance and symbolism.

Chinese opera is unique in many ways. It employs a complicated symbolism to portray human emotions and to express physical conditions and forms. The plots are based on stories from China's historical past, mythical legends and romances, but it is not possible to adequately recreate the scenes of old China on stage. Therefore innovative stage props and expressive gestures are a common characteristic of these plays.

The opera artist must fully demonstrate his or her feelings through song and movement. Gestures and actions are often made to signify certain inner emotions or desires and the opera artists have been trained in these since the age of seven. For example, at a particular point in a well-known play about a fisherman and his daughter, the fisherman stands a couple of metres from his daughter holding an oar. This means that the man is standing at one end of the boat while the daughter is at the other. The movement and action of the man and his daughter are so well coordinated that they appear to be rowing the boat on a perilous sea.

On a Chinese opera stage a horse may be represented by a horse whip

They then make gestures as if casting a big net and pulling in lots of fish. Later their actions also give the impression of adjusting the sails and anchoring their boat. Their skill in making the appropriate gestures captures the attention of the audience completely.

The facial features are used to indicate gestures of sorrow, happiness and other emotions. The hands and fingers may indicate the emotions. For example when an actor is angry he repeatedly shakes his right hand in distress. When he is in utter distress he swings his long pig-tailed hair in a continuous motion, to the admiration of the audience. The opera artist should have a light and agile step, something which is obtained after years of disciplined training. How fast he runs indicates his mood and intention. He has to be physically fit to move with the music as he sings and acts out his role.

6.2 | Music and instruments

The yangqin, a popular string instrument for Chinese opera.

Musical instruments accompany the singer on stage, and the music must synchronise with the voice and gestures of the opera artist. The three types of opera instrument are the percussion, the string and the wind and they are specially made for the various qiang diao 腔调 or the standard tunes, such as xipi 西皮 (west skin), erhuang 二黄 (two tunes) which are subdivided into daoban 倒板 (opposite), manban 慢板 (slow), yuanban 元板 (origin) and sanban 散板 (slow). Different instruments are used in certain standard civil 文 or military 武 plays. For the military plays the main musical instrument is the gu 鼓 . Other instruments used are the percussion instruments, made of copper and leather, such as the drums (gu 鼓), the gongs (daluo 大锣), the small gong (xiao luo 小锣), the cymbal (po 铍) and some wind insruments such as the bugler (hao tong 号筒) and the oboe (di 笛). For the civil plays the main instrument is a special guitar called the huqin 胡琴 . Other musical instruments are usually the stringed instruments made of bamboo such as the violin (hu qin 胡琴), the guitar (yue qin 月琴), fiddle (xian 弦), the flute (di 笛) and the clarinet (shao na 唢呐). Other musical instruments for the opera are the bones (ban 板), the cup bell (xing 星), the rattles (bangzi 梆子), the pan pipe (sheng 笙), and the two-stringed, three-stringed and four-stringed fiddles.

The qiang diao 腔调 is very important in Chinese opera because the entire performance can be spoilt by songs badly sung and out of tune. As mentioned earlier xipi and erhuang are often sung. Xipi is sung to express emotion or to relate an event while erhuang expresses

Some musical instruments

sadness and regret. Daoban is sung when a person wakes up from a dream or makes an outburst on hearing disappointing news. Manban is a harmonious tune and is pleasant to the ear. Yuanban is sung to express feelings and is sung at an even pace. Sanban is slow and is accompanied by the huqin (guitar) and the luo (gong). Other tunes sung on stage include liushui 流水, kuaiban 快板, banzi 板子 etc.

Musicians of the Chinese opera stage.

6.3 | Stages and props

During the Qing period or earlier a permanent imperial playhouse and an opera stage were constructed within the palatial complex for the entertainment of the imperial household. The Qing empress dowager, Ci Xi 慈禧 (1835–1908 AD) built an elaborate three-levelled opera stage in her Summer Palace in Beijing in masonry covered with a glazed tiled roof. Artists who performed there were considered honoured and were highly skilled.

A permanent Chinese opera stage is built of masonry materials such as traditional Chinese bricks. The stage floor is built of timber raised above the ground. It faces the audience. A temporary stage floor is raised a couple of metres above the ground and is built of timber but supported by a bamboo structural framework which is light and practical for transportation.

The stage is divided into front, back, right and left. The right is called shang chang men 上场门 while the left xia chang men 下场门. The central of the stage is called tai kou 台口. The right corner is named shang tai jiao 上台角 while the left xia tai jiao 下台角.

Symbolism plays a major role in Chinese opera in terms of prop and stage design, time and space as well as gestures and actions. It is usually not practical to bring real live animals or vehicles on stage. Therefore, furnishing and decoration are minimal and are represented by the simplest elements and gestures, movements and actions of actors are portrayed in certain

Chinese weapons used by Chinese opera artists.

symbolic ways that have been handed down for generations. For example, a horse is represented by a whip and how the actor holds and uses it signifies a particular action. He holds the whip in front and touches it with his left hand, then moves it backwards a little and swings it as he "mounts" the "horse".

The props are usually simply but artistically made to portray either the interior of a building, the exterior scenery and landscape. The interior space may be represented by a screen suggestive of a large space divided by many internal walls, a table and a couple of chairs to represent a well furnished hall. When the chair is placed in front of the table it suggests that the space is limited perhaps to the size of a room. But if the chair is placed behind the table the space may be a study or a magistrate's court. If the chair is placed on top of the table it may represent a high platform or a hill depending on whether the play is civil or military. The entrance of a traditional house or an individual room is supposed to have a threshold. It would be too complicated to lay a kerb on every occasion when an actor steps into a house or a room so he has to raise his foot as if stepping over a kerb when he enters the house. If he wants the audience to recognise that the door is closed he has to mime opening it.

In a military play all sorts of weapons are used in a fighting scene. Wooden weapons represent metal spears, tridents or swords. A chariot is represented by two flags with patterns of wheels. The liu, a stage assistant, holding the flags and appearing to push them, is the driver, while the passenger holds on to the flags. Usually wars are fought by the sea so the sea is symbolised by runners carrying white flags with wave patterns and strong wind is represented by waving black flags held by a number of liu characters. Tents may be set on fire and the fire is represented by flashing flame-like images made through lighting effects. Thunder and lightning is represented by flashing lights and beating of the drums and gongs. Scenery is portrayed by vivid landscape paintings on boards.

6.4 | Characters and stagehands

There are basically 7 types of stage character namely the male (sheng 生), the female (dan 旦), the supporting male (zheng 净), and the clown (chou sheng 丑生), supporting attendants (liu 流), martial assistants for good leaders (shang shou 上手) and martial assistants for the evil leader (xia shou 下手). The male artists or sheng range from old (lao sheng 老生), martial (wu sheng 武生) to young (xiao sheng 小生), depicting a cross section of society in terms of age and character. The females range from the young and beautiful (qingyi 青衣, the main actress) to the old and wise (lao dan 老旦). In a military play some male actors may have to play the role of a warrior (wu sheng 武生) and actresses the role of a female martial artist (wu dan 武旦 or dao ma dan 刀马旦). The zheng character usually wears a painted face and portrays a brave and robust man with a bass

Female actress in the initial stage of make up.

voice. Sometimes he is acrobatic like a wu sheng and holds weapons in his hands. Thus, the zheng is subdivided into tong chui 铜锤, jia zi 架子 and wu er hua 武二花. Tong chui sings with a loud, rich voice and holds the chui 锤 (a ball shaped hammer) in his hand. Jia zi also needs to sing well and he may or may not be a military character. Wu er hua is a martial artist who performs acrobatic feats. The chou sheng is usually the comedian in the play and he needs to have a sense of humour and delights

Female actress in the final stage of make up.

the audience with his wit and humour. Liu usually takes on the role of court or government office attendants or carriage drivers. Shang shou are followers of the upright military leaders while xia shou are followers of the evil leaders or outlaws.

Every character on stage is heavily made up and has his face painted with heavy eye make up. A xiao sheng has his face painted white but his cheekbones pink. His eyebrows are painted black and his eyes lined with heavy make up. The dan is also heavily made up. But the lao sheng and lao dan only use skin-coloured make up. The most striking face make up is worn by the zheng and his face colour scheme depends on the role he plays. For example, if he is upright and good he wears red. If he is shrewd and introverted he wears yellow. If he is brave and blunt he wears blue. If he is a spirit he wears green. The variety of face make up is so wide that it is impossible to list all of them. Some examples of face make up and the richly embroidered garments are illustrated in this and the following pages. The back stage workers are just as important as the actors or actresses because without them there will be no music or organisers who see that every scene is well set. These back stage workers are called ke 科. There are basically seven types of ke in an opera troupe, namely the musicians, the wardrobe managers, the wardrobe assistants, the make up artists, furniture arrangers, the assistant and general managers.

Because an opera artist may be required to play any role, a martial artist or a gentle scholar or even a clown, he has to be very versatile and

A qingyi or a young female opera artist and a xiao sheng or a young male artist

talented even though generally each artist will specialise in a particular role. He or she is also expected to know how to do his or her own make up and which garment to wear for a particular scene.

6.5 | Costumes and accessories

There are set rules regarding costumes and colour schemes. Yellow is worn by one who plays the role of an emperor or royal, red or purple for Mandarins and high ranking officials, blue for low-grade government officials, white for elders or those in distress and black for those of low birth. The elaborately sewn garments are based on styles which were fashionable during the Qing and Ming dynasties. The pattern and style of each garment indicates the rank and class of the character.

The countless types of garments are kept in 4 categories of storage box. The first stores clothes, for poor as well as rich characters and for female and male roles. The second stores garments and armoury for military figures. The third stores garments for imperial households and emperors. The fourth stores headdresses, armoury and fittings.

Headdresses are elaborate, especially those used by the main characters. Hats are classified into: lang mao (crowns for emperors), tian guan mao 天官帽 (hats for top officials), fang mao 方帽 (hats for civil government officers), yuan sha mao 圆纱帽 (hats for low grade officers) and zong mao 粽帽 (hats for wu chou, martial officers). Even the shoes are stylised because each character wears a particular type of shoes. For example, the xiao sheng wear a pair of high-soled boot-like shoes and the tan a pair of embroidered, flat-heeled shoes.

Types of Chinese opera weapons are also numerous. There are long and short weapons. The long weapons are chang qiang 长枪 (long staff), chang mao 长矛 (long spear), yue 钺 (long-handled axe), ji 戟 (staff and spear), shu 殳 (long wooden stick), cha 叉 (long handled fork) and pa 耙 (long handled rake). The short weapons are gong jian 弓箭 (bow and arrow), jian 剑 (sword), dun pai 盾牌 (shield), gang bian 钢鞭 (steel lash), dao 刀 (broad sword) and chui 锤 (metal ball with handle). Some weapons are used only by special characters. For example, the guan dao, the long-handled curved broadsword is only used by Guan Yu 关羽, a famous warrior of the Three Kingdoms era noted for his bravery and loyalty. These weapons are not made of metal but rather of wood, rattan or bamboo so that no one is in danger of being badly hurt. They are made to look like real weapons but are more decorative.

Equipment used on a Chinese opera stage is extensive. Some of the more important items are: the circular umbrella (used in an imperial court), tents, flags (representing carriages and water), oars (representing rowing boats), black flags (representing wind), yellow cloth (representing an imperial edict), seals, lanterns, umbrellas and fans.

Chinese opera costumes are fashioned upon Qing or Ming dynasty costumes

7  Chinese food and medicine

问刘十九

wèn liú shí jiǔ

白 居 易

bái jū yì

绿 蚁 新 醅 酒，

lù yǐ xīn péi jiǔ

红 泥 小 火 炉。

hóng ní xiǎo huǒ lú

晚 来 天 欲 雪，

wǎn lái tiān yù xuē

能 饮 一 杯 无。

néng yǐn yī bēi wú?

This poem by Bai Ju Yi describes cooking over a red clay stove and the comfort of having a drink by a stove (possibly with food nearby) in the evening with falling snow.

143

7.1 | Introduction

The theory of yin and yang is applied to all things Chinese including the classification of food and herbs. For over three thousand years the Chinese have combined the various ingredients for cooking food and the various types of food in harmonious balance for sustenance and the improvement of health. Since the 5th century BC they have discovered the secrets of using herbs and other natural ingredients for healing. The ancient records named Huangdi Neijing 皇帝内经 contains information on the anatomy of man, the causes of illnesses and the methods of healing. During the Three Kingdoms period the well known physician, Hua Tuo 华陀, was skilled in applying a form of anaesthesia for surgery. By the first century AD three thousand types of herbs were recorded in the Shennong Bencaojing 神农本草经 for curing ailments. Ming dynasty physician Li Shi Zhen 李时珍 contributed much to the development of Chinese herbal medicine by compiling his voluminous Bencao Gangmu on 1892 types of Chinese herbs. His writings were translated into many foreign languages after publication.

In the 5th century AD the Chinese discovered the meridian system in which zhenjiu 针灸 or acupuncture was used to cure ailments. The skill of using fine metal needles and inserting them into the meridian or nerve points of the patient requires many years of learning and practising the skill. There are 365 nerve points on the patient's body. Cure is achieved through stimulating the particular point that corresponds to the symptom of the illness. Presently, acupuncture is used for the healing of many illnesses including arthritis, asthma and all kinds of aches and pains. Very often it is used as a form of anaesthetic.

All forms of Chinese medical treatment are based on the theory of the balance of yin and yang and all things can be classified as yin or yang. For example, the upper part of the body is yang while the lower yin and the back yang while the chest yin. For all things to flourish there must be a combination and balance of yin and yang. Therefore, a person is healthy when his body system is in harmony as a whole and his organs are functioning well. If his body system is off balance in terms of yin and yang then he falls ill because yang sheng ze ri 阳盛则热 (too much yang leads to heat) and yin sheng ze han 阴盛则寒 (too much yin leads to cold). For example, ren shen 人参 is used to cure a weak constitution and to improve qi in the body system but it should not be misused or there will be ill effects such as bleeding. To remain healthy a person needs fresh air, exercise, nourishing food and a healthy mental condition. Thus, the Chinese pay a great deal of attention to the way food is cooked and a balanced diet is maintained to sustain and prolong life.

7.2 | Food

Chinese cuisine is a 3,000-year-old art based not only on skill and using the best quality ingredients but also on applying the ancient art of balancing the yin and yang qualities in the food. The Chinese classify each type of vegetable and meat in terms of yin and yang, and combine vegetables with meat in such a way that each cooked dish will be balanced. They know that food may be changed from one to the other depending on the way it is cooked. For example, a steamed fish is yin (cooling) but a deep fried fish is yang (heating).

The skill of balancing food was developed as early as the 16th century BC. A minister of the ruler of the Shang kingdom named Yi created Chinese cooking utensils and the art of cooking using the nature of the food to balance the diet. During the 5th century BC cooks began to create cuisines with medical values. In the publication called Huangdi Neijing 黄帝内经, a Warring States record, there are rules on how to regulate diet and improve the taste of food. The Han publication, Shennong Bencaojing 神农本草经, listed certain herbs and vegetables as being beneficial to the body. By the Song dynasty it was recorded that many diseases

Chinese art of eating
The table set for a Chinese dinner is covered with a clean table cloth. The bowls, cups, spoons etc. are placed in an artistic presentation. Chopsticks are used to carry the food. For a big table a central turntable is used to rotate the dishes and make the food easily within reach. It is Chinese etiquette for the hostess to offer food to the guests by bringing it to their dishes.

could be cured through proper diet and eating the right food. The development of cooking skills and lists of food for curing ailments intensified during the Jin, Yuan and Qing dynasties.

Different foods were classified according to their perceived nature. They might be han 寒 (cold/yin), liang 凉 (cool/yin), ping 平 (neutral), wen 温 (slightly warm/yang), and ri 热 (hot/yang). Han and liang foods were believed to reduce fever, relieve thirstiness and coughs while wen, warm foods reduce running noses, headache etc. The five tastes of food are sour, sweet, bitter, hot and salty. Sour food relieves diarrhoea, asthma and other ailments. Slightly sweet food relieves ailments connected

with the veins. Bitter food helps to cure an overheated body system. Hot food helps blood circulation and salty food helps to stop diarrhoea.

Han food includes bitter gourd, lotus, water melon, suger cane, tomato, banana, dong gourd, yellow gourd, snail, crab etc. Liang food includes luobo 罗卜, sigua 丝瓜, pocai 波菜, maize, green bean, bean curd, orange, apple, pear, duck egg, abalone, frog's leg, mushroom etc. Han and liang food such as abalone regulates the liver function because it cools the yangness in the system. Hot food is chilli, pepper and other foods with a hot taste. Wen food includes apricot, ginger, spring onion, onion, papaya, glutinous rice, wine, vinegar,

Herbal chicken 御膳富贵鸡
The photograph shows (at the centre) a Chinese herbal chicken delicacy called baked chicken with multiple herbs. There are 8 treasured herbs (4 yin and 4 yang) in the dish. This dish gives tonic to the blood and it benefits the brain and relieves fatigue.

Fish and herbs 怀药芫爆鱼丝
The photograph shows how fish can be cooked with herbs to reduce blood sugar in the body system.

almond, dates, venison, prawn, fish, chicken meat, beef, goat meat, liver, ham, etc. Wen and hot food such as apricot stimulates blood circulation and nurtures the heart and lungs. The neutral or ping food includes rice, sweet potato, flat bean, yellow bean, black bean, red bean, red carrot, ground nut, lotus seed, corn, pomfret, fruit, pork, goose meat, frog meat, butter and milk and these foods nourish the spleen and balance the digestive system.

Knowing the nature of individual foods enables the Chinese to eat the proper food to nurture the various internal organs, balance the yin and yang and enhance the qi of the body. For example, to nurture the stomach they believe one should eat carrots, melons, apples and vegetables. To nourish the spleen one can drink honey and drinks made from herbs prescribed by a Chinese medicine shop. The most harmless food is the neutral, including certain vegetables, fruit and egg white. In ancient writings lists of food for the nurturing of various parts of the body are found. A short list is given below.

Food	Parts of body that benefit from the food
lotus fruit	ears
lizi (fruit)	spirit or energy
liver	eyes
abalone	eyes
wang xian (a fish)	bones
deer meat	kidneys
apple	spleen
apricot	heart
bean	intestines
catfish	kidneys
wine	blood vessels

Wine has always been regarded by the Chinese as a necessity at an important dinner such as that held on the eve of the Chinese new year or to celebrate a wedding. It is not within the scope of this book to research the making of wine, but it is worth mentioning the various types. There are basically 3 types, namely yellow wine, white wine and putao wine 葡萄酒 . The yellow wine contains 20% alcohol, the white 40 to 60% while the putao 葡萄 may be up to 40%. The art of cooking in China formalised at the stone age about 7000 or 8000 years ago. The variety of Chinese food served in China as well as in other parts of the world where there are Chinese residents is countless. The style of cooking can be broadly classified in 7 styles namely Lucai 鲁菜 (northern or Shandong), Sichuan 四川, Guangdong 广东, Beijing 北京, Huaicai 淮菜, Kongcai 孔菜, Sucai 素菜 (vegetarian). Lucai originated from Shandong during the Western Zhou dynasty. Its speciality is the liyu 鲤鱼 (carp) cooked in a great variety of styles. It can be steamed, barbecued, fried, poached, deep-fried or double boiled.

Sichuan dishes are usually hot and suitable on a cool day, as Sichuan is a cool part of China. Guangdong is the favourite cuisine of the Cantonese and includes a wide variety of dishes. It has a 2,000 year history and includes dishes cooked with pigeons, snakemeat, chicken, beef, venison and even special worms such as dongchong 冬虫. Huaicai originated about 1,000 years ago and is noted for its refined and exquisite presentation. Beijing cuisine started in the northern part of China, combining the style of Shandong cooking with other tribal cookery to make it distinctive. Its

Scallops with ladybell root 玉参美蓉干贝
The photograph shows a Chinese delicacy called quick-fried egg white with scallops, polygonatum and ladybell root. This dish is cooked with the herb Yu Zhu and Sha Shen (poygonatum and ladybell root). It improves the complexion and nourishes the lung (yin manifests as dry coughs and chronic coughs). This dish promotes the production of body fluid such as saliva etc.

Egg plant 松塔茄子
The photograph shows (at the centre) a dish of braised egg-plant with pine nuts. The egg plant can prevent hardening of blood vessels. It is a cool energy food, thus it clears internal excess heat. Pine nuts retard aging and they moisturize the lungs and lubricate the intestines.

Chinese desserts.

most popular dishes are probably the famous Beijing duck and its lamb dishes. Kongcai dishes were originally created in the imperial courts to delight the royalty and so they are elaborate in style and exquisitely presented. Sucai or vegetarian food is now very popular outside China because they are nutritious and are meat-free and low in cholesterol.

7.3 | Maintaining good health

The Chinese doctor believes that prevention is better than cure and so the maintenance of harmony in the body system is essential to good health. Qi or energy is maintained through daily exercise, nourishing food and rest. Qi is obstructed if the circulatory system or the circulation of blood is hampered. In this case the person's lungs and other organs in the body will be affected and symptoms such as excessive perspiration, poor eyesight and breathlessness will result. Qi can also be hampered by outbursts of temper, stress and frustration. The Chinese have always recognised the importance of maintaining the inner peace of mind as well as the outer physical strength for the sustenance of long life. They have created all forms of martial exercises such as the Taiji Quan and Qigong for the maintenance of harmony of the body system. They believe in taking regular meals and regular exercise for the prevention of illness rather than allowing health to deteriorate and then taking drugs to aid recovery.

It is believed that everything can be classified under the Five Elements, Gold, Wood, Water, Fire and Earth, and the internal organs of a man can also be classified as follows:

Gold: large intestines, nose and lungs
Wood: gall bladders, eyes and livers
Water: bladders, ears and kidneys
Fire: small intestines, tongues and hearts
Earth: spleens, mouths and stomachs

The Five Elements react with one another harmoniously or antagonistically. Thus Wood controls Earth, Fire controls Gold, Water controls Fire, Earth controls Water and Gold controls Wood. Therefore, an ailment of the large intestine affects the gall bladder while the stomach affects the bladder. On the other hand, the saying "pei tu sheng jin" 培土生金 (improve Earth to develop Gold) means that if the spleen is strengthened then the lungs will also be made healthier since the workings of the Elements are such that Wood gives life to Fire, Fire to Earth, Earth to Gold, Gold to Water and Water to Wood. Another example is that the liver (Wood) governs the working of the spleen (Earth) because of their elements. The workings of the Five Elements are a means to ensure and double check nature's way, or the interrelationship of things in nature, to prevent excess or insufficiency.

The organs can also be classified under yin or yang as follows:

Yin: liver, spleen and kidneys
Yang: gall bladder, small intestine, stomach, heart and bladder

In knowing the nature of the organs and the nature of the herbs or medicine the doctors are able to induce a balance in the person's system. The Chinese believe that if a person is ill he must be examined using the following procedure: wang 望 (look), wen 闻 (listen), wen 问 (ask), qie 切 (feel the pulse). Wang (look) involves the close examination of the patient in terms of his spiritual and mental wellbeing, the colour of his face and the colour of his tongue. Wen (listen) means the doctor listens to the voice and senses the breath of the patient. Wen (ask) is finding out about the patient's eating habits and his overall physical form. Qie (feel the pulse) requires the doctor to feel the pulse of the patient to diagnose the illness.

The heart is one of the most important organs in the body as it circulates the blood to the entire body. If a person suffers from a heart ailment he looks pale and weak and his tongue appears very red. The liver is closely related to the gall bladder. If a patient suffers from excessive yang in his liver or gall bladder his eyes may be bloodshot and he may have constant headaches. If a patient suffers from too yang a stomach he may have heartburn and indigestion. If a patient coughs hard and has difficulty in breathing he may be suffering from lung problems. The above examples show that the illnesses and their symptoms can be detected from the external physical form through the Chinese approach to healing the sick.

The Chinese believe that illnesses can have external causes and environmental influences including feng shui which they classify as liu

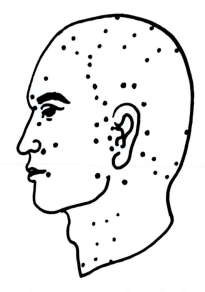

It may be surprising to learn that to heal an ailment needles are used to activate the primary channels or meridians of the body. For example, to cure a headache acupuncture needles are put in the foot of a patient to relax him. The meridians of a human head are shown in the diagram below.

yin 六淫 namely the wind风, the cold寒, the heat 暑, the dampness 湿, the dryness 燥 and the fire 火 (foul air). Illnesses can also be caused by the upset of the internal motions such as happiness 喜, anger 怒, worry 忧, anxiety 思, unhappiness 悲, fear 恐 and fright 惊. Thus, it is advisable for a person to avoid being caught in a hostile environment or in a constantly stressful situation because many of the fatal illnesses are caused by adverse environmental and emotional factors. To cure such illnesses the first principle is to help the patient regain his sense of wellbeing in terms of harmony within his body system and harmony with reference to the built environment.

Illnesses can also be caused by the clogging of qi. There are 6 types of qi namely men qi 门气, jing qi 精气, jin qi 津气, ye qi 液气, xue qi 血气 and mai qi 脉气. Men qi circulates through the pores of the skin. Jing qi is the essence or spirit. Jin qi circulates through the body secretions while ye qi through the body fluids. Xue qi and mai qi are in the blood. If the qi in the body is blocked the person falls ill. To cure him the doctor has to bring about balance and harmony in the body system through herbs or acupuncture.

The Chinese also believe in maintaining good health through taking regular bu 补 (repair) food such as tonics made with deer antlers, bezoar (gall bladder of the rhinoceros, sea horse, birds' nests etc). Some tonics are even good for appearance. For example, he shou wu 何首乌 (polygonum multiflorum) is supposed to bring life to white hair and turn it black.

7.4 | Herbs

The Chinese way of healing an ailment is not just to detect the cause of the ailment from one symptom. It is based on the study of the patient as a whole being and achieving balance and harmony in the physical as well as the mental aspects. Therefore, how the patient reacts in a particular environment, climate and weather is of much importance in the assessment of his health. The herbist examines the spirit, the energetical condition and the feeling of the patient before he prescribes herbs for a cure.

Chinese Herbs
The slide above shows ten types of Chinese herbs for the reduction of "heatiness" (a too yang condition for the body). The herbs are placed as shown, complete with pin-yin and English names.

甘草 gan cao radix glycyrrhizae	淅贝母 zhi bei mu bulbus fritillariae thunbergii	麦冬 mai dong radix ophiopogonis	玄参 xuan shen radix scrophulariae
荆芥 jing jie herba schizonepetae	薄荷 bo he herba menthae		杷叶 pa ye folium eriobotryae
黄芩 huang qin radix scrutellarae	连翘 lian qiao frutus forsythiae		金银花 jin yin hua flos lonicerae

Seahorses, cardycap, birdnests and horn.

Chinese herbs may be classified under one of the four types namely han 寒 (cold and yin), ri 热 (hot and yang), wen 温 (luke-warm and yang), and liang 凉 (cool and yin). Herbs can also be classified according to their tastes such as suan 酸 (sour), ku 苦 (bitter), gan 甘 (slightly sweet), xing 辛. If the patient's body system is too yang and he suffers from high fever he may use herbs to reduce the yang. Some herbists believe that yin chen hao 茵陈蒿 (artemisia capillaris), chai hu 柴胡 (bupleurum falcatum) which are good for the bladder and the laxatives ma huang 麻黄 (epedra sinica), baimao 白茅 (imperata cylindrica), jingjie 荆芥 (schizonepeta tenuifolia) and dahuang 大黄 (rheum officinale) can 'qing' 清 or clear and cool the system. On the other hand if the patient is too yin he may neutralise the yin to a balanced state.

It is very important that a patient consults a Chinese herbist or doctor and have his illness diagnosed before trying a herbal cure. The combination of herbs and the quantity of each herb used should be prescribed by the doctor. The above prescription is only for general guidance.

There are basically 7 approaches towards prescribing herbs. For serious illnesses the da fang 大方 using strong herbs is prescribed. But for minor ailments xiao fang 小方 using mild herbs is used. For the improvement of health over a period of time huan fang 缓方 is prescribed. But for urgent cases such as severe diarrhoea ji fang 急方 is used for a quick cure. Qi fang 奇方 is prescribed for special cases to cure particular illnesses. Ou fang 偶方 using two herbs, is used to cure some ailments that require the elimination of two toxins in the body system. Fu fang 复方 is prescribed repeatedly to get rid of an unwanted imbalance in the system.

Herbal medicine is made in various forms. It can be in pills which are made from dry herbs first pounded in powder. For example, for curing a patient whose system is too yang the liuwei dihuang wan 六味地黄丸 is used. Many nutritious herbs are suitable for making wine tonics. The most common of the herbal soups for the improvement of health is the four-gentlemen soup, si jun zi 四君子. The above herbs mentioned in each form of herbal cure are carefully blended in ratios or quantities specified by specialists. All recommended forms of herbal cures mentioned here are to be taken prescribed by physicians and are not to be taken without consulting a doctor.

7.5 | Prolonging life

The Chinese saying "ren dao qi shi gu lai xi" 人到七十古来稀 (it is rare to find a man of 70) suggests that longevity is not common and cannot be expected. Since time immemorial the Chinese have been searching for the secret of longevity. The first emperor, Qin Shi Huang Di 秦始皇帝, spent much of his court physicians' energy in searching for the pill of immortality so that he could live forever. Similarly, the Tang rulers ordered alchemists and herbists to research the use of metal compounds and herbs in producing pills of immortality. Numerous medical experts in that era had written on the secrets of longevity through cultivating a healthy lifestyle and habits. Sun Si Miao 孙思邈, a well known medical expert, advocated that if one were to prolong life one should value his health above wealth and fame, one should not be too emotional and too indulgent on food. Similarly, Qing dynasty physician, Cheng Zhong Ling 程钟龄, echoed Sun's thinking and advised that the moderation and regulation of the intake of food, the sustenance of energy and qi in the body and the avoidance of being excessively emotional contribute to longevity. Another Qing physician, Gao Shi Shi 高世斌, revealed that too much emotional upheaval (including extreme happiness) could adversely affect the function of the heart. It was also believed that too much worry could affect the lungs, sadness and anxiety could cause ill effects on the spleen and too much anxiety and fear could adversely affect the heart and liver. The Chinese always advocate that one should always be "xin ping qi he" 心平气和 (heart and qi at peace) in order that the body functions well. Habits, such as eating nutritious food regularly, going to bed early and getting up early, that help to improve health should be cultivated. Positive thinking, being inquisitive, courageous and optimistic leads to longevity.

The Chinese believe that the wellbeing of a person is achieved through mental and physical good health. A healthy diet should be balanced, consisting of meat and lots of vegetables cooked with limited salt and occasionally with vinegar. There should be an adequate fluid intake but little sugar. There should be plenty of rest and little worry. It is always better to take regular exercise and lots of walks. Bad habits such as smoking and drinking should be avoided. Emotional stress should also be avoided by talking about one's worries and confiding one's worries in trusted friends, forgetting failures and forgiving others.

Physical health is sustained through eating nutritious food in moderation. Li Shi Zhen's Ben Cao Gang Mu 本草纲目 contains countless recommendations on quality food for consumption. For example, yellow beans are rich in proteins and low in cholesterol. Therefore, bean curds, bean sprouts and drinks made from beans are good for the health. Sesame oil helps the flow of qi and strengthens bones whereas red beans are believed to nurture the spleen. Carrots, unpolished rice and many types of fruit are rich in vitamins and should be eaten regularly.

Medical cabinet for herbs
The Chinese take much pride in carving the names of the herbs on the front drawers of the medicine cabinets.
This photograph shows an excellent example.

Epilogue

Chinese culture is so rich and multifaceted that it would take more than a lifetime to acquire knowledge of all of its forms and appreciate the splendour and wisdom of its philosophy. As the Chinese saying goes, "xue wu zhong zhi" 学无终止 (there is no end to learning). This book does not attempt to cover the full spectrum of Chinese culture but rather to give an interesting introduction and perspective to the most illustrious facets and encourage readers to read further into each and every area of Chinese culture. It is hoped that the reader would continue to search for spiritual nourishment and wisdom through further study and discover the fascinating roots of Chinese culture.

Reading through the pages of this book, it becomes clear that Chinese culture is deeply interwoven in individual human lives as it pervades and informs the family unit, clan association, etiquette, events in life, festivities, beliefs, martial exercises, architecture, landscaping, various aspects of arts and craft and food. The Chinese saying "bao luo wan you" 包罗万有 (it has every variety of thing) can certainly be applied to Chinese culture. It has spanned 5,000 years and spread over a huge geographical area within and outside China.

There are Chinese migrants in every corner of the world and so Chinese culture is not practised in China alone. It is believed that quite often a traditional overseas Chinese adheres to his cultural roots more than a native Chinese. However, the younger generations of overseas Chinese who have grown up outside China may not have the benefit of the wisdom derived from a sound understanding of Chinese culture. It is hoped that this book will remind future generations about some of the philosophies and skills developed by their forefathers.

With the rapid developments in science and technology and the interaction between East and West, Chinese culture may one day be integrated with modern practices and concepts of living. For example, there may be differences between the ways the East and West practise medicine but there is great advantage in integrating the best of the two systems to cure a very sick patient. Western medicine may be used to eliminate an infection and Chinese herbs may be taken to strengthen the patient's physical constitution through the fine tuning of the body system.

It is not possible to sum up Chinese culture in a book. The sign of the taiji illustrates the basic philosophy behind Chinese thinking because it is a symbol of perfect equilibrium reflecting the essence of balance between body and mind. The black area symbolises the yin quality while the white yang. The yin is always becoming the yang and the yang is continually tending towards yin and the two exist in perfect harmony.

Addendum

Qigong-The Art of Gaining Internal Strength
Introduction

Qi in Chinese means breath and gong is skill, technique and art. Qigong is the Chinese art of gaining strength internally. Through this art the internal organs of the body are "exercised" and, in doing so, become more healthy and resistant to illnesses. Through this technique of using breathing to massage the internal organs and activate the blood circulation of these organs good health is maintained and life prolonged. The word qi written in Chinese consists of the words that suggest the steaming of rice while the word gong is made up of two words, gong and li. Gong in this case means work and li means strength. So the word qigong literally implies that to attain success in this exercise one must use breath (although not steam) in such a skillful manner that strength of internal organs is achieved through breathing exercises. The Chinese sums up this by four words: yiyi yong qi which means "use your will to move the circulation".

There are many ways of practicing this three thousand-year-old art of qigong. Some, called jinggong, are seen to be passive as the participants are seen to be in meditation. Some, called donggong, are active and the participants move their hands and limbs in rhythm. Some are seen as a combination of both jing and donggong. Generally, the art of qigong can be classified under four styles namely: dao (Daoist), fo (Buddhist), kong (Confucian) and Taiji and Weitan (related to martial arts) etc.

Another Chinese saying, qi xing xue xing which means if qi is circulated blood to is circulated. Therefore, diseases that arise because of poor blood circulation can be eliminated through the training in qigong. Qigong not only activate blood circulation it also calms the nerve. The ancients in China had long since discovered that nervousness and stress are harmful to the body. Calms one's nerves and circulates

159

one's blood for better health. Similar to acupunctural treatment through qigong the meridian points in the body are stimulated by the activation of qi.

Although qigong is known to bring about good health, cure illnesses and improve complexion, however, it must be learnt correctly under an experienced trainer. If it is practiced incorrectly it may lead to poor health and illnesses, both mentally and physically. Incorrect practice leads to zuo huo ri mo (bringing vicious illness through inappropriate practice).

Qigong Related to Martial Movements

The most difficult of all the donggong qigong is the Wuqin qigong (five animal qigong). It is an advanced form of qigong created by the taiqi experts. When the practitioner perform this art he or she makes vigorous movements imitating one of the following animals: the bear, the monkey or the tiger. This style of qigong should not be practiced without proper guidance from a master and it is too advance to be introduced in this book. The aim of this addendum is an introduction to qigong exercises for beginners. Therefore, the following section discusses the various steps of the Taiji qigong.

General Training for Qigong Exercises

Like all other exercises one must not do qigong if one has taken a meal less than an hour ago or one is ill (even a cold). Immediately after the exercise one should not wash one's hands or body or eat a hearty meal. Before one starts training on qigong one may even emprove one's physical well-being and stamina by doing the following exercises: (a) breathing exercises and (b) building up one's chuanjia (strength int he arms and legs) by swinging-the-arms (Say for 20 minutes) daily.

Qigong Breathing

Learn to do qigong breathing by the following way: Breath in a relax manner but through the nose and into the lungs as well as the abdomen. Breath in and out regularly. Concentrate your thoughts and thing of the diantian (the area an inch below the navel). When one swings one's arms one should relax and stand firmly on the ground. By doing this simple exercise one builds up one's strength in the legs and arms.

Taji Qigong

In doing the Taiji Qigong one should remember the following: (a) do not use force; (b) be relax; (c) breath naturally and move slowly; and (d) make sure the movements are continuous.

A

Step 1 (see diagram A)

While exhaling stand erect in a relax posture and look ahead. Put your hands down and hold them at your sides. Keep the tip of your tongue touching the upper palate. Yiyi yongqi (use your will to activate the qi in your diantian by thinking of your diantian).

B

Step 2 (see diagram B)

Bend your knees and, while inhaling, raise your arms in level to the shoulder. The palms remain downward. At the same time concentrate on your qigong breathing.
Repeat Step at least five times.

Step 3 (see diagram C)

Bring your arms to your chest and stand up straight. Stretch out your palms and arms. While exhaling, turn your palms downward and push them down to the knee level as you breath in. Repeat this step ten times.

C

161

Step 4 (see diagram D)

   While exhaling bend your body on the left. Stand on your right foot and raise your right arm over your head Your right palm faces downward while your left palm upward and level with your shoulder.
   While breathing in reverse step 4. This means the right palm faces upward and so on. Keep on repeating step 4 and 5 for ten times and keep on doing the qigong breathing.

D

Step 5

   Stand on two feet and bend them slightly. Bring down both arms. Palms are turned inward. Stand erect and bring arms up with you palms turning outward. Do not forget your breathing exercise at the same time. Repeat this step ten times.

Step 6 (see diagram E)

   Stand firmly with bent knees and arms. Then stretch out your left arm. Turn your waist to the right and at the same time push your left palm (at the level of your ear) toward and over the right palm, your eyes looking at the right. Reverse this by stretching out your right arm and turning your waist to the left and so on.
Repeat this ten times while you breath in and out.

E

Step 7 (see diagram F)

Bend over forward, relax your shoulder and let your hands fall downward. Turn your arms in circular manner, up and down while you breath. Do this ten times.

Step 8 (see diagram G)

While exhaling stand firmly on the left foot and free the right. Keep your left hand by the side and, while inhaling, swing your right arm to the left like as if your palm is holding a ball. Reverse the step by swinging the left arm. Repeat this ten times.

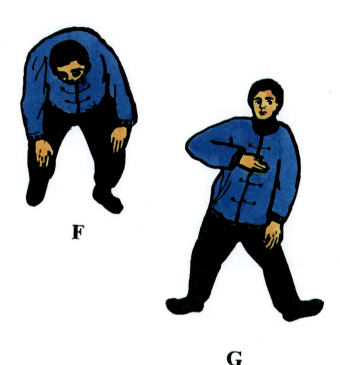

F

G

Step 9

Stand in a relax manner and put your hands by the side. Swing your hands and turn your waist to the left and then to the right while you exhale. Your eyes follow your palm. Reverse your movement while you inhale. Repeat this ten times.

Step 10

Bend your knees slightly and hold your fists with fingers facing in. Place your fists next to your waist. Inhale and turn your waist to the left while you push out with the right fist. As you push you open your fist into a palm. Exhale when your body returns to its original

position. Reverse the exercise and repeat the entire step ten times.

Step 11

Remain standing with your legs slightly bent. Bring your left palm up to the level of the eye. Your right palm is level to your waist. Move your palms up and down forming circular movements. Exhale as you reverse the actions by raising your right palm first. Repeat this step ten times.

Step 12 (see diagram H)

Put forward your right leg and bend it slightly. Inhale as you stretch out you hands with your palms turning from outward to inward. Lean forward with your eyes looking slightly downward and your arms slowly moving down and crossing one another and to the knee level. Reverse the action by raising your head so that it faces upward. Exhale while you stretch out your arms upward. Repeat this step ten times.

H

Step 13

Bring back your arm by your side and in the front. Your arms slightly bent and your palms face outward. Put you weight on your right leg and your left foot forward as you inhale. Your body and your palms gently push forward as you exhale. Repeat this ten times.

Step 14

Straighten your arms with your palms facing one another. The weight of your body is mainly on your right foot. Inhale as you stretch your arms outward and then inward as you exhale. Your weight is centered on your left as you stretch your arms. Repeat this ten times.

Step 15

Stand on both feet and hold your fists by the sides but palms upwards. Push forward your right fist as you inhale. Bring it back by the waist and exhale. The push forward your left fist and inhale. Exhale as you bring back your fist. Repeat this ten times.

Step 16

Stand up straight with your arms level with your shoulder but your palms downward as you exhale you bend down, body straight. Inhale while you bring your body and arms up. Repeat this ten times.

Step 17

Stand up but turn to the left as you make arcs of movement with your outstretched arms in an anti-clock wise direction. Inhale. Reverse the movement and move your arms in a clock wise direction. Exhale. Repeat this ten times.

Step 18

Stand up and put your left foot slightly forward. Move right palm like as if it is hitting a bouncing ball. Inhale. Reverse the action and exhale. Repeat this ten times.

Step 19

Stand with knees slightly bent. Move your palms upward in front of you as you inhale. Exhale as you push your palm down. Repeat this ten times. The above Taiji Qigong exercises are excellent preparation before you practice Taiji Chuan which consists of 108 continuous movements made up of some of those described above.

Index

BOOKS BY AUTHOR, Dr. Evelyn Lip, PH.D (Arch)

Lip, Evelyn, Feng Shui: A layman's Guide, Heian International, Inc. Torrance, CA., USA, 1987.

Lip, Evelyn, Feng Shui For the Home, Heian International, Inc. Torrance, CA., USA, 1990.

Lip, Evelyn, Feng Shui and Design of Logos, Trademarks and Signboards, Heian International, Inc. Torrance, CA., USA, 1998.

Lip, Evelyn, Feng Shui For Business, Heian International, Inc. Torrance, CA., USA, 1990.

Lip, Evelyn, Personalize Your Feng Shui, Heian International, Inc., Torrance, CA., USA, 1997

Lip, Evelyn, Choosing Auspicious Chinese Names, Heian International, Inc., Torrance, CA., USA, 1992.

Lip, Evelyn, Feng Shui, Chinese Colours and Symbolism, Singapore Institure of Architects Journal, Singapore, July, 1978.

Lip, Evelyn, Geomancy and Building, Development and Construction, Singapore, 1977.

Lip, Evelyn, Chinese Temples and Deities, Times Books International, Singapore, 1981.

Lip, Evelyn, Island and Water, Times Books International, Singapore.

Lip, Evelyn, Fun With Chinese Horoscopes, Graham Brash, Singapore, 1981.

Lip, Evelyn, Chinese Temple Architecture in Singapore, Singapore University Press, Singapore 1983.

Lip, Evelyn, Chinese Beliefs and Superstitions, Graham Brash, Singapore, 1984.

Lip, Evelyn, Chinese Customs and Festivals, Macmillan Education, London.

Lip, Evelyn, Notes on Things Chinese, Graham Brash, Singapore, 1988.

Lip, Evelyn, & Lim, Bill, Architectural Detailing in the Tropics, Singapore University Press, Singapore, 1988.

Lip, Evelyn, Feng Shui, Environment's of Power, Academy Editions, London, 1995.

Lip, Evelyn, What is Feng Shui, Academy Editions, London, 1997.

PATERNAL FAMILY

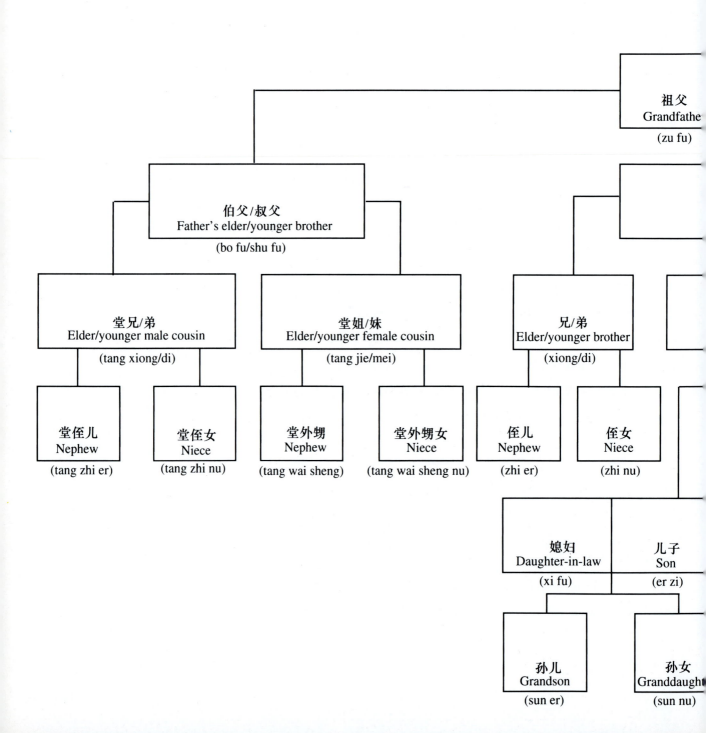

祖父
Grandfather

(zu fu)

伯父/叔父
Father's elder/younger brother

(bo fu/shu fu)

堂兄/弟
Elder/younger male cousin

(tang xiong/di)

堂姐/妹
Elder/younger female cousin

(tang jie/mei)

兄/弟
Elder/younger brother

(xiong/di)

堂侄儿
Nephew

(tang zhi er)

堂侄女
Niece

(tang zhi nu)

堂外甥
Nephew

(tang wai sheng)

堂外甥女
Niece

(tang wai sheng nu)

侄儿
Nephew

(zhi er)

侄女
Niece

(zhi nu)

媳妇
Daughter-in-law

(xi fu)

儿子
Son

(er zi)

孙儿
Grandson

(sun er)

孙女
Granddaughter

(sun nu)

OF _____

(name of reader)

祖母
Grandmother
(zu mu)

姑妈/姑姐
Father's elder/younger sister
(gu ma/gu jie)

姐/妹
Elder/younger sister
(jie/mei)

姑表兄/弟
Elder/younger male cousin
(gu biao xiong /di)

姑表姐/妹
Elder/younger female cousin
(gu biao jie/mei)

外甥
Nephew
(wai sheng)

外甥女
Niece
(wai sheng nu)

表侄儿
Nephew
(biao zhi er)

表侄女
Niece
(biao zhi nu)

表外甥
Nephew
(biao wai sheng)

表外甥女
Niece
(biao wai sheng nu)

女儿
Daughter
(nu er)

女婿
Son-in-law
(nu xi)

外孙
Grandson
(wai sun)

外孙女
Granddaughter
(wai sun nu)

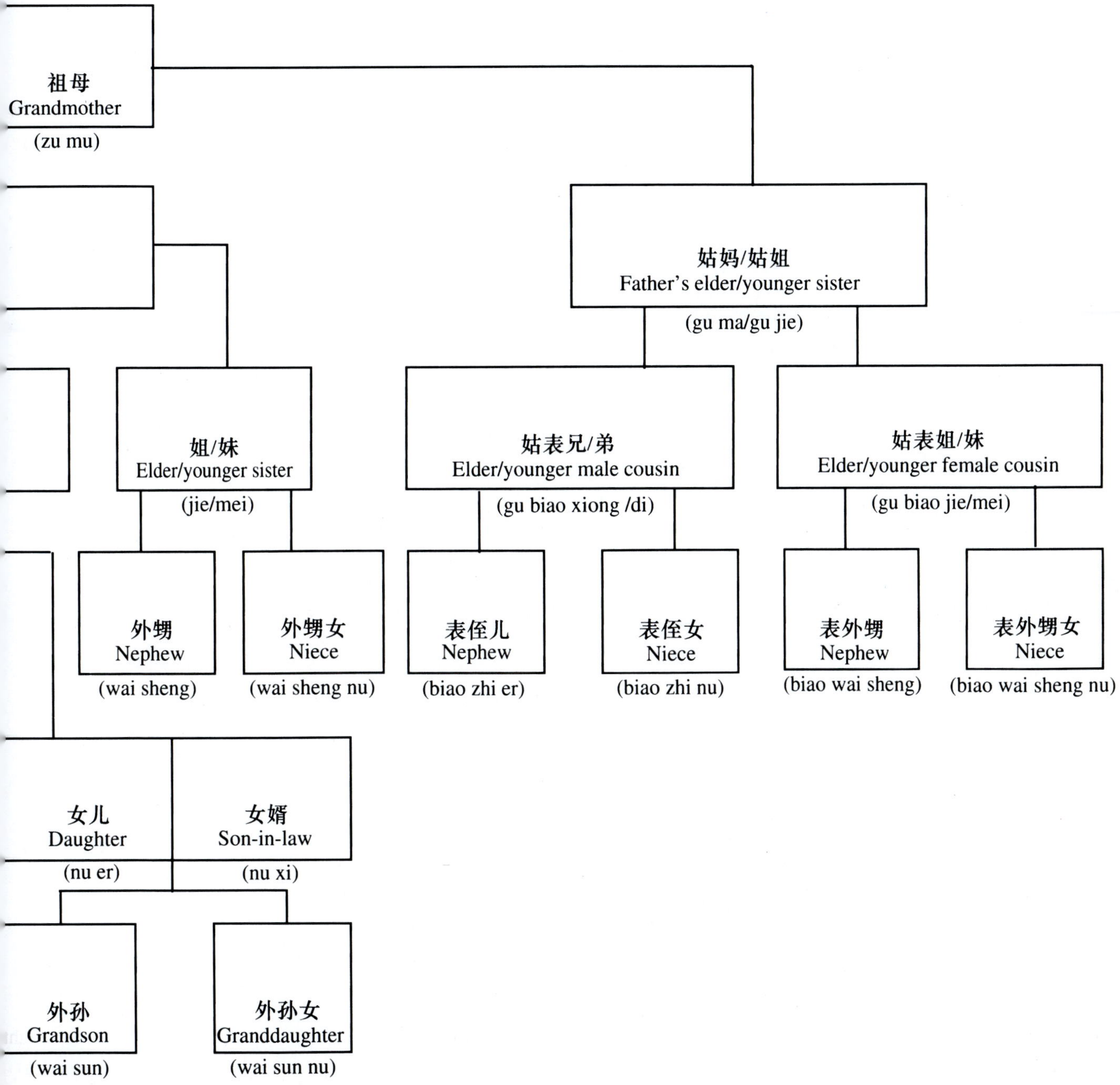

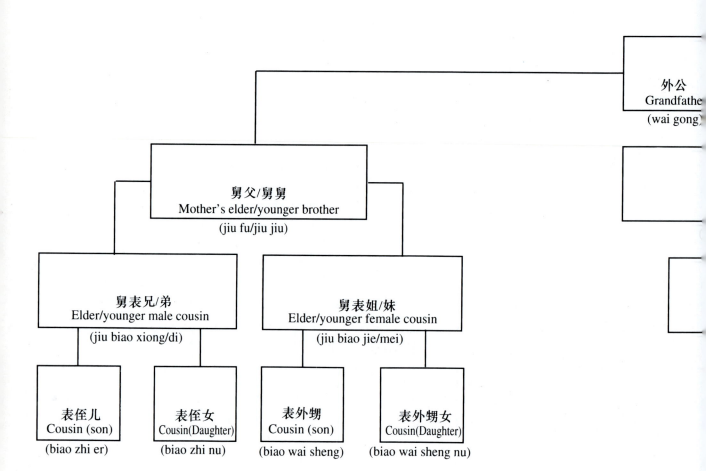

外公
Grandfathe
(wai gong

舅父/舅舅
Mother's elder/younger brother
(jiu fu/jiu jiu)

舅表兄/弟
Elder/younger male cousin
(jiu biao xiong/di)

舅表姐/妹
Elder/younger female cousin
(jiu biao jie/mei)

表侄儿
Cousin (son)
(biao zhi er)

表侄女
Cousin(Daughter)
(biao zhi nu)

表外甥
Cousin (son)
(biao wai sheng)

表外甥女
Cousin(Daughter)
(biao wai sheng nu)

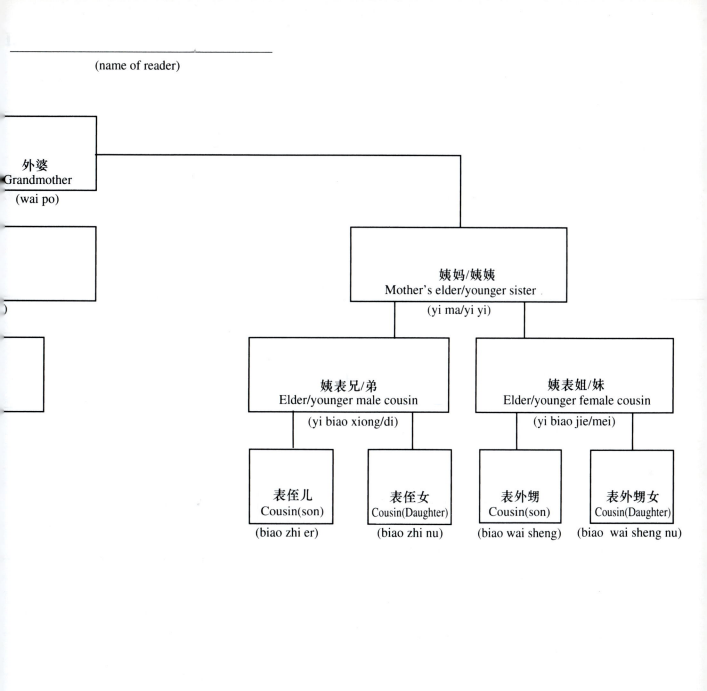

(name of reader)

外婆
Grandmother
(wai po)

姨妈/姨姨
Mother's elder/younger sister
(yi ma/yi yi)

姨表兄/弟
Elder/younger male cousin
(yi biao xiong/di)

姨表姐/妹
Elder/younger female cousin
(yi biao jie/mei)

表侄儿
Cousin(son)
(biao zhi er)

表侄女
Cousin(Daughter)
(biao zhi nu)

表外甥
Cousin(son)
(biao wai sheng)

表外甥女
Cousin(Daughter)
(biao wai sheng nu)

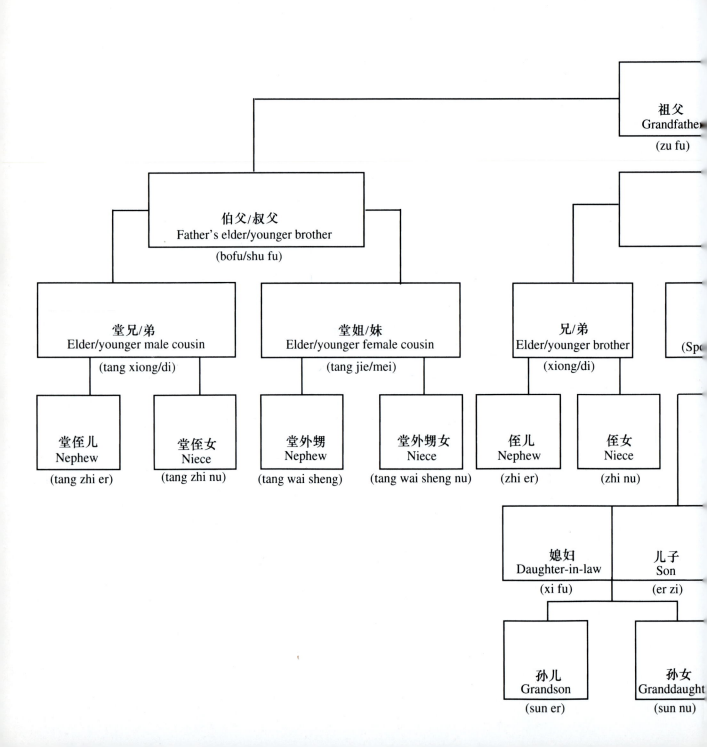

祖父
Grandfather

(zu fu)

伯父/叔父
Father's elder/younger brother

(bofu/shu fu)

堂兄/弟
Elder/younger male cousin

(tang xiong/di)

堂姐/妹
Elder/younger female cousin

(tang jie/mei)

兄/弟
Elder/younger brother

(xiong/di)

(Sp

堂侄儿
Nephew

(tang zhi er)

堂侄女
Niece

(tang zhi nu)

堂外甥
Nephew

(tang wai sheng)

堂外甥女
Niece

(tang wai sheng nu)

侄儿
Nephew

(zhi er)

侄女
Niece

(zhi nu)

媳妇
Daughter-in-law

(xi fu)

儿子
Son

(er zi)

孙儿
Grandson

(sun er)

孙女
Granddaught

(sun nu)

REE OF ______________________

(name of reader's spouse)

祖母
Grandmother
(zu mu)
姑妈/姑姐
Father's elder/younger sister
(gu ma/gu jie)
ame)
姐/妹
Elder/younger sister
(jie/mei)
姑表兄/弟
Elder/younger male cousin
(gu biao xiong/di)
姑表姐/妹
Elder/younger female cousin
(gu biao jie/mei)
外甥
Nephew
(wai sheng)
外甥女
Niece
(wai sheng nu)
表侄儿
Nephew
(biao zhi er)
表侄女
Niece
(biao zhi nu)
表外甥
Nephew
(biao wai sheng)
表外甥女
Niece
(biao wai sheng nu)
女儿
Daughter
(nu er)
女婿
Son-in-law
(nu xi)
外孙
Grandson
(wai sun)
外孙女
Granddaughter
(wai sun nu)

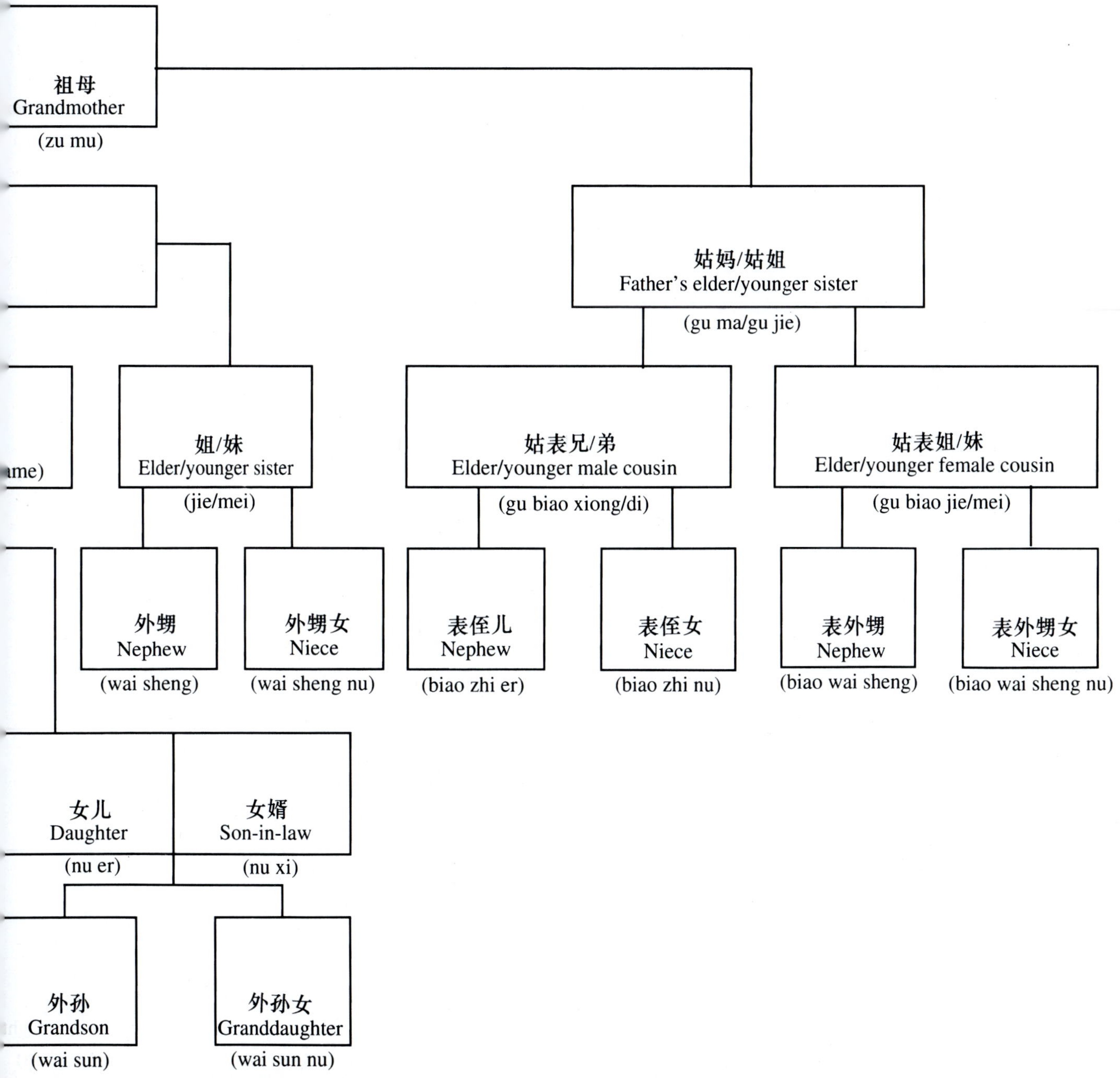

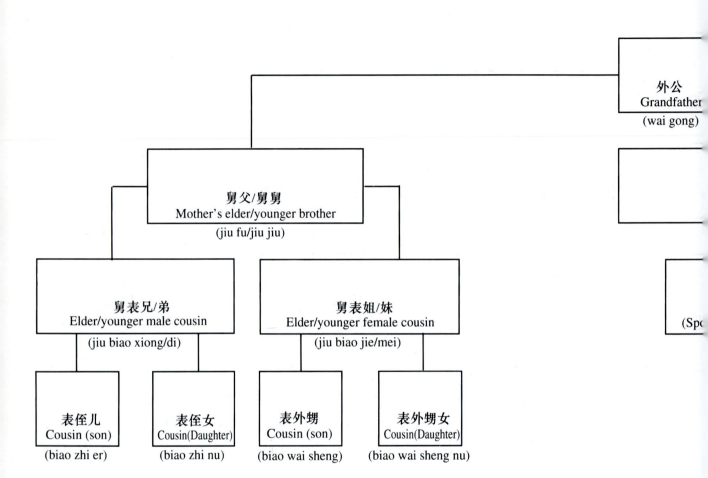

外公
Grandfather
(wai gong)

舅父/舅舅
Mother's elder/younger brother
(jiu fu/jiu jiu)

舅表兄/弟
Elder/younger male cousin
(jiu biao xiong/di)

舅表姐/妹
Elder/younger female cousin
(jiu biao jie/mei)

表侄儿
Cousin (son)
(biao zhi er)

表侄女
Cousin(Daughter)
(biao zhi nu)

表外甥
Cousin (son)
(biao wai sheng)

表外甥女
Cousin(Daughter)
(biao wai sheng nu)

(Sp|

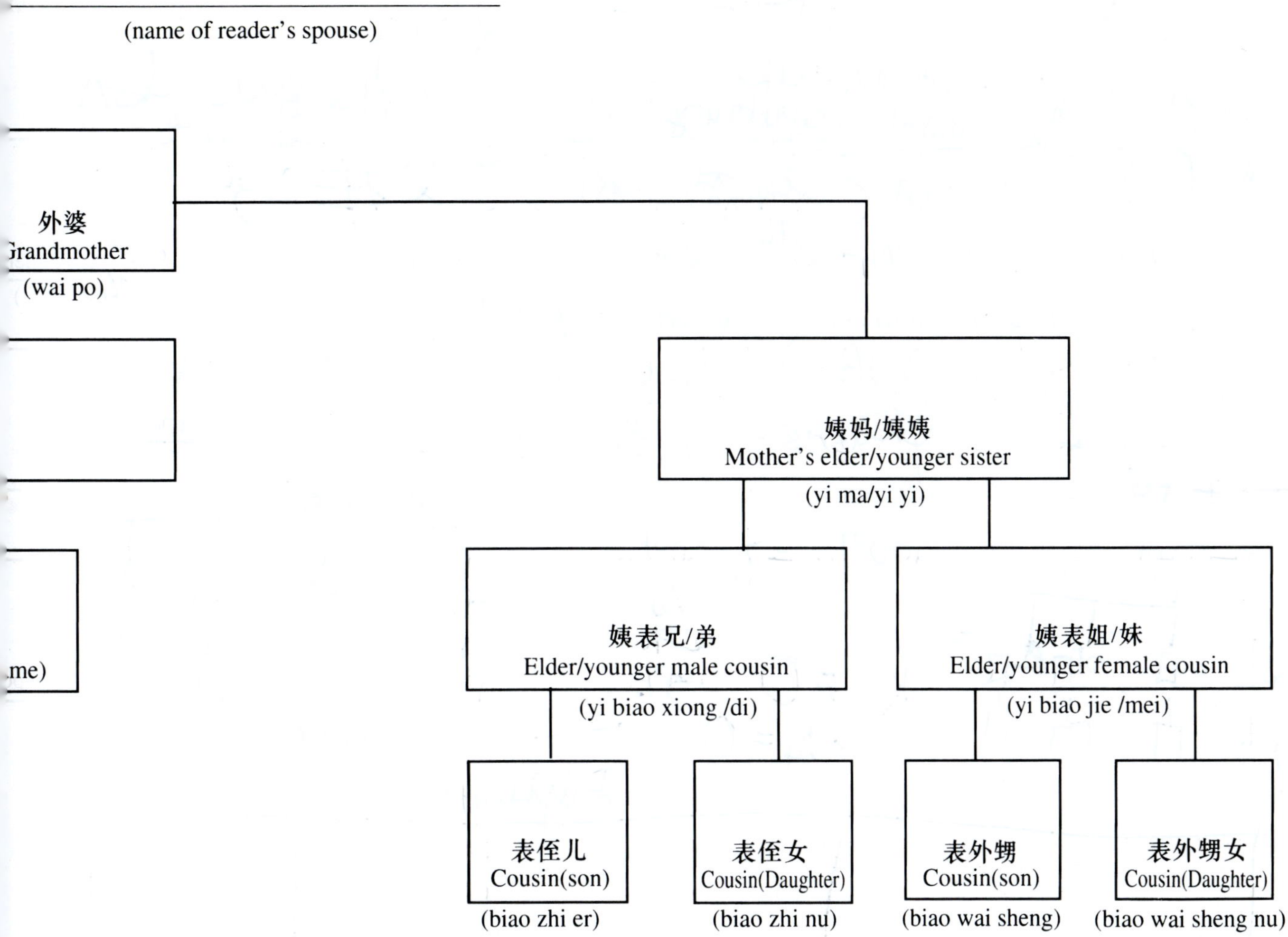

_____

(name of reader's spouse)

外婆
Grandmother
(wai po)

(me)

姨妈/姨姨
Mother's elder/younger sister
(yi ma/yi yi)

姨表兄/弟
Elder/younger male cousin
(yi biao xiong /di)

姨表姐/妹
Elder/younger female cousin
(yi biao jie /mei)

表侄儿
Cousin(son)
(biao zhi er)

表侄女
Cousin(Daughter)
(biao zhi nu)

表外甥
Cousin(son)
(biao wai sheng)

表外甥女
Cousin(Daughter)
(biao wai sheng nu)

TREE NOTES 2014

Hypothesis ?
Probability of Intellectual & Moral Capability on

GLOBAL USA culture.

"Jutila Zai Jia 2014..." 父 生 口 3

Graciana · 2014 fall — 26th August

Kazuang & Tzein
Kenny + Jacquelin

Indiana University online"

KENYA   PROBABILITY Bio 106 || Zhang — CHINA
♀ + ♂

$100\% = 2$ (50%)

$\frac{1}{2}$
25%

$\frac{1}{2} = \neq 0$ .4%

$\frac{1}{4} = 0$

Same

Duplicate

Mono Culture
Bi Culture or/and ?
Poly culture

THESIS :—
→ Observation / Research / visibility Study
→ quantative / qualitative data ?
www. Analystation / World Agroforestry / Lake victoria / Org
→ Papers / Books / Articles / magazine

NOTES

NOTES

NOTES

NOTES

NOTES

NOTES